Essential Histories

The Seven Years' War

Essential Histories

The Seven Years' War

Daniel Marston

OSPREY PUBLISHING
Bloomsbury Publishing Plc

Kemp House, Chawley Park, Cumnor Hill, Oxford OX2 9PH, UK
1385 Broadway, 5th Floor, New York, NY 10018, USA
29 Earlsfort Terrace, Dublin 2, Ireland
Email: info@ospreypublishing.com

OSPREY is a trademark of Osprey Publishing, a division of
Bloomsbury Publishing Plc

First published in Great Britain in 2001

Osprey Publishing is a division of Bloomsbury Publishing Plc

Printed and bound in India by Replika Press Private Ltd.

21 22 23 24 25   20 19 18 17 16 15 14

A CIP catalogue record for this book is available from the British Library

ISBN: 978 1 84176 191 6

Editorial by Rebecca Cullen
Design by Ken Vail Graphic Design, Cambridge, UK
Cartography by The Map Studio
Index by Alan Thatcher
Picture research by Image Select International
Typeset in Monotype Gill Sans and ITC Stone Serif
Origination by Grasmere Digital Imaging, Leeds, UK

The Woodland Trust
Osprey Publishing is supporting the Woodland Trust, the UK's leading woodland
conservation charity, by funding the dedication of trees.

www.ospreypublishing.com

Contents

Introduction

The causes of the Seven Years' War are rooted in the outcome of an earlier conflict, the War of the Austrian Succession (1740–48). The Treaty of Aix-la-Chapelle, which brought this war to an end, had done nothing to assuage the anger of Austria over the loss to Prussia of the wealthy province of Silesia. Nor had it been able to contain the conflicting colonial ambitions of France and Britain, which provoked continued skirmishing well beyond the official cessation of hostilities. The Seven Years' War was, therefore, essentially a continuation of the War of the Austrian Succession, but it was different from its predecessor in two significant ways.

The first important difference was that the Seven Years' War was truly a global war, requiring a total commitment of resources on the part of all combatants. In the long term this meant that, because countries were putting all they had into simply continuing to fight, any gains became secondary. In the extreme, it meant that a country such as Prussia was fighting for her very survival.

Queen Maria Theresa of Austria. (Anne S.K. Brown Military Collection, Brown University Library)

The second major difference was a definitive shift that occurred in alliances that had existed for most of the first half of the eighteenth century. Austria and Britain, long-time allies, broke their treaties and Austria sided with France, formerly her enemy. Prussia, in turn, broke her ties with France and sided with Britain, although this alliance too was broken, eventually leaving Britain with no allies on the continent.

The principal combatants in the Seven Years' War were Austria, led by Queen Maria Theresa; Britain, led by George II and later George III (also Electors of Hanover); France, with Louis XV on the throne; Prussia, led by Frederick II (later known as Frederick the Great); and Russia, with Empress Elizabeth.

Frederick II of Prussia. (Anne S. K. Brown Military Collection, Brown University Library)

Chronology

1755 9 July Braddock's defeat

1756 15 January Convention of
Westminster
1 May First Treaty of Versailles
17 May Declaration of war between
France and Britain
28 May Surrender of British at
Minorca
29 August Prussian invasion of
Saxony
1 October Battle of Lobositz
17 October Saxon army surrenders

1757 11 January Russia signs First Treaty
of Versailles
1 May Second Treaty of Versailles
6 May Battle of Prague
18 June Battle of Kolin
23 June Battle of Plassey
26 July Battle of Hastenbeck
9 August Fort William Henry
capitulates
30 August Battle of Gross-Jägersdorf
September British raids on French
coast
8 September Convention of Kloster
Zeven
5 November Battle of Rossbach
5 December Battle of Leuthen

1758 2 June Fall of Fort St David
June–September British raids on
French coast
8 July Battle at Fort Carillon
(Ticonderoga)
1 August Louisbourg capitulates
3 August First British contingent
arrives in Germany
25 August Battle of Zorndorf
27 August Fort Frontenac is sacked
14 October Battle of Hochkirch
24 November Fort Duquesne is
abandoned

13 December Siege of Madras

1759 17 February Siege of Madras is lifted
23 July Battle of Paltzig
24 July Fort Niagara capitulates
26 July Fort Carillon is abandoned
31 July Attack on Montmorency
Falls
1 August Battle of Minden
12 August Battle of Kunersdorf
18 August Battle of Lagos
4 September Dresden is captured
13 September First Battle of the
Plains of Abraham
20 November Battle of Quiberon
Bay

1760 22 January Battle of Wandiwash
28 April Second Battle of the Plains
of Abraham
23 June Battle of Landeshut
31 July Battle of Warburg
15 August Battle of Liegnitz
8 September Montreal surrenders
9 October Raid on Berlin
16 October Battle of Kloster Kamp
3 November Battle of Torgau

1761 7 June Island of Dominica surrenders
15-16 July Battle of Vellinghausen
30 September Capture of
Bunzelwitz

1762 5 January Death of Empress
Elizabeth
12 February Island of Martinique
falls
2 or 5 May Treaty of St Petersburg
24 June Battle of Wilhelmsthal
10 August Fall of Havana
6 October Manila is captured

1763 10 February Treaty of Paris
15 February Treaty of Hubertusburg

Old enemies, new friends

North America

New France (the French colonies in North America, a large portion of present-day eastern Canada) and the 13 British colonies had been engaged in colonial conflict since 1608. Tensions escalated in 1747 when the colonies of Virginia and Pennsylvania formed the Ohio Land Company in the Ohio River valley, encouraging British traders to cross the Allegheny Mountains and establish trading posts. The French, feeling that this territory lay within their sphere of influence, began a process of establishing posts along the Ohio and Mississippi rivers to contain this British expansion. In 1753 the French deployed 3,000 men into the region to build forts and take offensive action as necessary.

George II of Great Britain. (Anne S. K. Brown Military Collection, Brown University Library)

In response, Governor Dinwiddie of Virginia dispatched a major of the Virginia Militia, George Washington, to deliver a declaration to the French commanders at the newly built forts of Presque Isle and Le Boeuf, which stated that these were on Virginian territory and should therefore be vacated. The French did not comply and Dinwiddie pushed for the British to build their own forts in the region to support trading claims. In 1754 a party of 40 men was sent to build Fort Prince George, on the site of present-day Pittsburgh. The French appeared, seized the men, and sent them back to Virginia. They claimed the fort as their own and renamed it Fort Duquesne. A further attempt in the summer by Major George Washington and 300 colonial troops was also turned back after a battle near Fort Necessity on 2 July 1754.

Following this defeat, the British decided in September 1754 to dispatch two regular army regiments to deal with the French in the Ohio River valley. They also sent £10,000 and 2,000 muskets to North America to raise more local colonial troops, in the hope that this would force the French to back down over the land issue. The British reinforcements sailed in January 1755, and a British naval squadron followed, under orders to stop any French ships attempting to reinforce New France. However, the French sent a fleet of 5,000 regulars, which succeeded in slipping past the Royal Navy blockading force, and by June had arrived in North America.

In June 1755 a British expeditionary force set out to seize Fort Duquesne. This force, commanded by Major-General Edward Braddock, was made up of two regular regiments, the 44th and 48th Foot, and various colonial detachments. The troops may have been regulars, but they were not well suited to the environment in which

New France and the British colonies

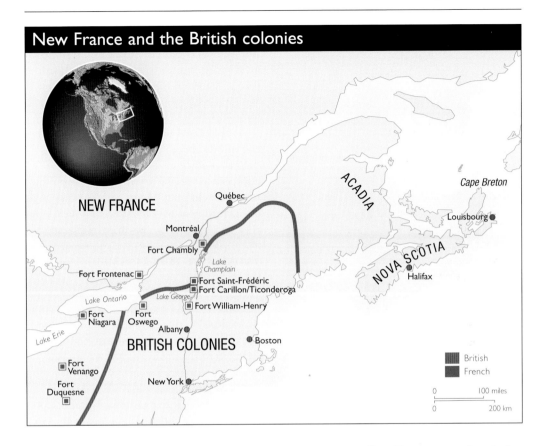

NEW FRANCE

Québec

Montréal

Fort Chambly

ACADIA

Cape Breton

Louisbourg

Lake
Champlain

Fort Frontenac

Fort Saint-Frédéric
Fort Carillon/Ticonderoga

NOVA SCOTIA

Halifax

Lake Ontario

Lake George

Fort William-Henry

Fort
Niagara

Fort
Oswego

Lake Erie

Albany

BRITISH COLONIES

Boston

Fort
Venango

New York

Fort
Duquesne

| | British |
| | French |

0   100 miles

0   200 km

they were being asked to fight. They had been trained in the linear continental tactics of the 1700s, but now had to operate in the thick forests of North America. The French units defending Fort Duquesne had a few regular companies, 100 men from the French colonial troops (Marines), 200 French-Canadian militia and 900 French-allied Native Americans.

On 6 July, a few miles from Fort Duquesne, the forward units of the British, led by Colonel Thomas Gage, met a larger force of French with their Native American allies. The British army in North America was unused to fighting in wooded terrain and had not been trained in the techniques suited to forest warfare. They had deployed, as much as they could in the surroundings, in the linear continental style, and had expected that their enemies would do the same. The French were able to cause considerable damage to the lead British columns while suffering little themselves, by using skirmishing tactics. Braddock reinforced the forward units with more troops, but with

little apparent effect. They attempted to deploy in linear formation. A British officer noted: 'The French and Indians fired from one position and then ran to a new position, while the British line remained in close quarters and fired from left to right as volley after volley fell within its ranks' (Journal of a British Officer, pp. 50–51). After two hours of fighting, the British began to retreat. Of the 1,370 British men, only 459 had not been wounded during the fighting. The French casualties have been estimated at three officers killed, four officers wounded, and fewer than 10 French regulars or militia killed or wounded. The French-allied Native Americans are estimated to have lost 100 men.

The other two campaigns of 1755 involved British provincial units against the French in the Lake George and Fort Niagara regions. Both sides moved troops into these regions in an attempt to seize vital strategic areas for future campaigns. The British were successful at Lake George on 8 September, but could only occupy the southern area of Lake

Empress Elizabeth of Russia. (Anne S. K. Brown Military Collection, Brown University Library)

George as the provincial troops were near mutiny. The British provincials sent against Fort Niagara were turned back at Fort Oswego as their commander, Governor William Shirley of Massachusetts, felt the French presence in the region was too strong.

India

The war in India had its roots in the commercial competition between the French East India Company and the English (British) East India Company. Since the early 1600s, both companies had been trading successfully on the Indian subcontinent. However, by the mid-1700s, the old Mogul Empire was rapidly being torn apart by internal strife, and both companies saw the potential advantages in the changing political situation. When war broke out in Europe in the late 1600s and early 1700s, the small trading posts in India were caught up in the fighting, although these engagements were on a much smaller scale than those in Europe or North America. Both companies raised local military forces of native Indians and local Europeans. The French had been

especially successful during the War of the Austrian Succession in raising and training local Indian troops. They seized the British post at Madras during this war, although it was later returned to the British in exchange for Louisbourg in North America in 1748.

As in North America, the fighting in India continued between the two rival companies even after peace treaties had been signed in Europe in 1748. The conflict also took on the added dimension of Indian princes siding with one company or the other in return for favors. However, in 1754 the British government, recognizing that tensions had escalated, dispatched the 39th Foot to Madras to serve as the backbone of the British military forces in the region. The fighting on the Indian subcontinent over the course of the following six years was a mix of company European and Indian (Sepoy) troops and regular troops, although the company troops on both sides far outnumbered the regular troops.

The colonial rivalry had pushed Great Britain and France towards war and both realized that they needed European allies in the event of a continental war. The stage was set for negotiations among the major powers of Europe.

Political dimension

Many of the participants in the Seven Years' War viewed the Treaty of Aix-la-Chapelle in 1748, which ended the War of the Austrian Succession, as a temporary truce. Austria had lost the valuable province of Silesia to Prussia; Prussia wished to defend her newly gained province and had aspirations of further expansion at Austria's expense. Great Britain and France were at odds in the colonies of North America and on the Indian subcontinent. All sides between 1748 and 1756 embarked on a series of treaty negotiations that would see the old alliances of the War of the Austrian Succession disbanded. The end product was the Convention of Westminster and the two Treaties of Versailles. (These treaties will be considered in more detail later in the

Louis XV of France. (Anne S. K. Brown Military Collection, Brown University Library)

chapter.) Russia was the new power to enter the fray during this period.

Each country brought her own specific aims to the bargaining table. Austria sought the reconquest of Silesia from Prussia, and Prussia's reduction to a minor state within central Europe. Great Britain wanted to fight a decisive colonial war against France in North America and India. The Achilles' heel of this colonial strategy was the Electorate of Hanover, which Great Britain wanted to safeguard from French and Prussian

aggression. The British realized that if Hanover was seized, any future peace settlement would mean relinquishing conquered French territories overseas in exchange for its return. France for her part also wished to engage the British in the overseas empire game, and recognized the benefits of seizing Hanover. The Prussians wished to hold on to their gains from the War of the Austrian Succession, and

India

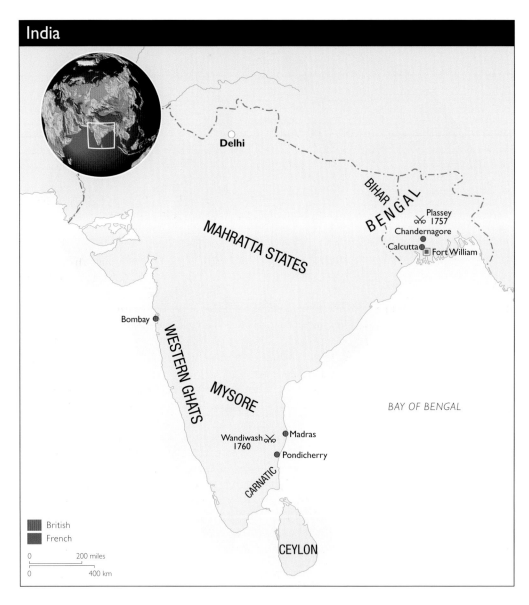

to seize Saxony if possible. Russia wished to curtail the powers of Prussia, fearing a Prussian plan to seize the Kurland region, and had plans for conquest in Poland and East Prussia.

Each country had her spies and ambassadors working behind the scenes, trying to gain the upper hand in negotiations. France and Prussia had renewed an existing defense treaty on 29 May 1747 that was to remain in force for 10 years. However, Prince Kaunitz of Austria was appointed ambassador to France in 1750. He remained in France for three years

and made valuable contacts in the French government. Upon his return to Austria, he became chancellor of state. Kaunitz saw the value of a potential Franco-Austrian alliance in seizing Silesia. The treaty negotiations were hurried and major changes occurred to the diplomatic map of Europe due to the rising hostility between France and Great Britain in North America in 1754.

Great Britain viewed Prussia and France as the greatest potential aggressors in another European war, and sought Russia as a possible guarantor of Hanover. Britain saw war in

Europe as a major obstacle to her strategic war plans in the colonies, and preferred the status quo to be maintained. She wished to engage the French overseas while Europe remained at peace. With an army that was small by European standards, Britain planned to utilize her troops in overseas theaters rather than remaining in Europe to safeguard Hanover. Britain and Russia negotiated a treaty on 30 September 1755 whereby Russia agreed to provide 55,000 troops and 40 galleys. The British in return agreed to provide a £100,000 subsidy per annum, with an additional payment of £400,000 if troops were moved from Russia to Hanover.

Frederick II, recognizing the formidable possibility of an Anglo-Austrian-Russian alliance against him, made overtures to the British government in May 1755, indicating that he had no designs on Hanover and wished for peace. Negotiations began between Prussia and Great Britain for a defensive treaty, and on 15 January 1756 the Convention of Westminster was signed. Both parties agreed to mutual aid in keeping foreign troops out of the German states. Prussia also hoped that the British would put pressure on the Russians not to mobilize against her.

Austria, however, did not wish to maintain the status quo. She wished to attack and humiliate Prussia and seize Silesia, and felt that the British had betrayed their long-time partnership by siding with Prussia. Realizing that this new alliance also left France isolated, Austria openly stated that she was negotiating with the French and that Great Britain should not object. Britain, in turn, hastened to explain to Austria that the Convention was defensive in nature.

The Russians were not sitting idly by. In April 1756, the Russians had five objectives: to begin the business of curtailing the powers of the King of Prussia; to engage Austria to assist in this endeavor; to mollify France to keep her from moving against Vienna; to promote a favorable situation in Poland, so that Russian troop movements across Polish territory would not be hindered; to keep the Swedes and Turks silent and inactive. Austria

began negotiations with Russia at this point. The subsidy treaty between Great Britain and Russia had not yet been ratified and seemed to be unnecessary in the aftermath of the Convention.

On 1 May 1756 the First Treaty of Versailles was signed between France and Austria. The significant agreements of this first treaty were that Austria would remain neutral in the event of an Anglo-French war; and that France would not attack any of Austria's territory. Austria would not assist Great Britain in a colonial war. Another provision of the treaty stated that if either country were attacked, 24,000 troops from the other would be sent as aid. The idea was that if France attacked Hanover, then Prussia would attack France, thus allowing the Austrians to move into Silesia.

While both the Convention of Westminster and the Treaty of Versailles were intended as defensive in nature, each also clearly had an offensive component. Russia was not a signatory due to French fears of Russian expansion into Poland. France had a close relationship with the Elector of Saxony, Augustus III, who was also the King of Poland, and both feared that Russian troops operating against Prussia would seize Poland and cause destruction in the area. France considered herself a major player in Poland and was unwilling to lose her position in the region. After extensive negotiations among Saxony, France, and Austria, a deal was reached. Although it was not concluded until the war had begun, by the end of 1756 the French had replaced the British as subsidy providers to Russia, and the Russians had promised not to meddle in the domestic affairs of Poland and to march across Poland with minimum damage.

Although the Russians were not an original signatory of the First Treaty of Versailles, Frederick II of Prussia realized that the walls were closing in on him. He saw a potential three-pronged attack on his territory, with the French attacking from the west, the Russians from the east and the Austrians from the south.

Linear and irregular warfare

Warfare in the Seven Years' War

The flintlock musket was the chief weapon of all armies during the Seven Years' War. It had been introduced at the beginning of the eighteenth century. It was not an accurate weapon – its accurate range was about 200–300 paces – but accurate fire was not its intended role. The musket was a quick-firing weapon when compared to the previous technology, and the concept for its use was for infantry units to approach along a given line of advance and deliver a devastating volley at close range, then reload to fire another volley. The amount of firepower and the ability to deliver it became the keys to success in battle.

Use of the new musket drew army formations out into longer lines, greatly extending the frontage of battle. At the Battle of Leuthen, the Austrian frontage was 4.5 miles (7.2km), while the Prussian frontage was just over 2 miles (3.2km) long. The Prussian frontage was smaller due to the tactic of the oblique order, which will be considered later. A common practice was to have one battalion of infantry deployed with two or three artillery pieces on its flanks. The artillery

Frederick's military instructions illustrating the oblique order. The idea is to deploy a large force on the enemy's flanks. This is done in secrecy as the first line is deployed in the normal linear formation opposite the enemy. Meanwhile, troops from the second line wheel around to the flank. See the map of Leuthen on p.41 for a demonstration of this tactic in the field. (Bodleian Library)

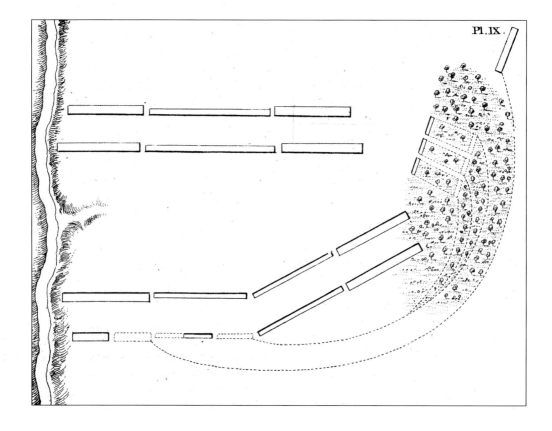

Pl.IX.

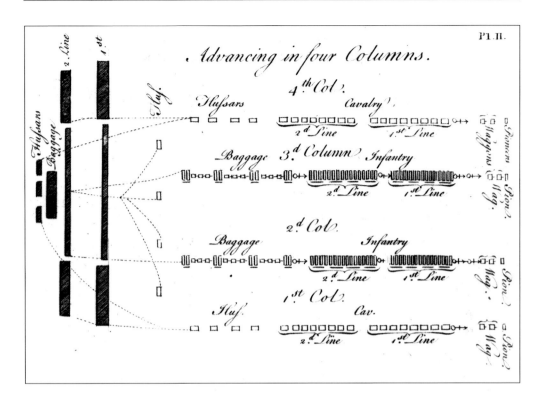

This image illustrates the complicated maneuver of deploying from column into battle line (continental style). (Bodleian Library)

pieces gave added firepower, but also provided a dividing line between infantry battalions.

The various armies of the Seven Years' War deployed in different levels of frontage. At times the Prussians deployed in three ranks of men, but due to casualties over the course of the war this dropped to two. The Austrians deployed in three ranks after the Battle of Kolin, which simplified firing techniques in the line and increased the flexibility of the units in battle. The British began the war with regiments deployed in three ranks, but by 1759 they were deploying in ranks of two.

This style of warfare required training in deploying for battle and marching across open or closed country. As lines were formed, generals attempted either to outflank the enemy or to inflict a devastating frontal attack. The armies usually deployed in two or three long lines of disciplined infantry and cavalry. The second and/or third lines would be used as reinforcements or in a flanking attack.

Discipline in battle was paramount under this system. Soldiers had to be trained to march over country in columns that would keep cohesion regardless of the terrain.

Upon reaching the enemy, troops would then have to deploy quickly into linear battle formation. Armies that failed to deploy were often defeated, as when the Prussians inflicted a heavy defeat on the Franco-German army at Rossbach by attacking while the Franco-German army was still marching in column formation.

Even when both armies were properly deployed in linear formation, maintaining discipline was still important to all the men on the field. Troops were required to maintain cohesion under a barrage of enemy artillery and musket fire, not firing until ordered to do so. Initially, a platoon fire system was developed for the various armies. The first series of drills was very complicated and difficult to carry out. To illustrate with a simplified example: each battalion was divided into three lines, and then into eight firing units. Each unit – designated a platoon – would either fire in a sequence from the center out to the wings of a line, or vice versa, or simultaneously. All commanders understood that after three volleys the troops fired at will, thus keeping up a continuous fire. The Prussians, due to their level of training and discipline, were the closest to achieving the ideal system. Other armies would adopt a simplified version of this system, where the first rank of men would fire a single volley, followed by the second rank and so on as each rank reloaded. The British applied this tactic well at the Plains of Abraham in 1759.

Each army attempted to inflict a devastating volley that would disperse the enemy. The attack would sometimes proceed in straight lines due to the terrain. However, commanders often attempted to take an enemy line on the flank: if they succeeded in breaking through a flank, they could cause the enemy to lose cohesion all along the front. Cavalry were employed as, for the

most part, shock troops who would exploit an exposed flank of the enemy.

Terrain often influenced deployment on the battlefield. At Kunersdorf, the Russians deployed in a swampy area dissected by ravines that required the Prussians to deploy to battle in a very small frontage, which in turn allowed the Russians a smaller target to hit with artillery. In heavily wooded or hilly terrain, large linear formations had a difficult time marching and deploying for battle. The British army in North America suffered initially against the woodland tactics of the French and their Native American allies, and in similar circumstances the Austrians inflicted

An artist's impression of linear warfare. The troops in the forefront are arrayed in two lines, with artillery marking the boundary between units (location of forward artillery indicated by clouds of smoke). Cavalry is deployed to the right flank. (Anne S. K. Brown Military Collection, Brown University Library)

heavy losses on the Prussian army with their irregular or light infantry and cavalry.

Each army of the Seven Years' War had strengths and weaknesses in dealing with the various tactics listed above. During the course of the war, some armies reformed and learned from defeat, while others acknowledged attributes but failed to apply them.

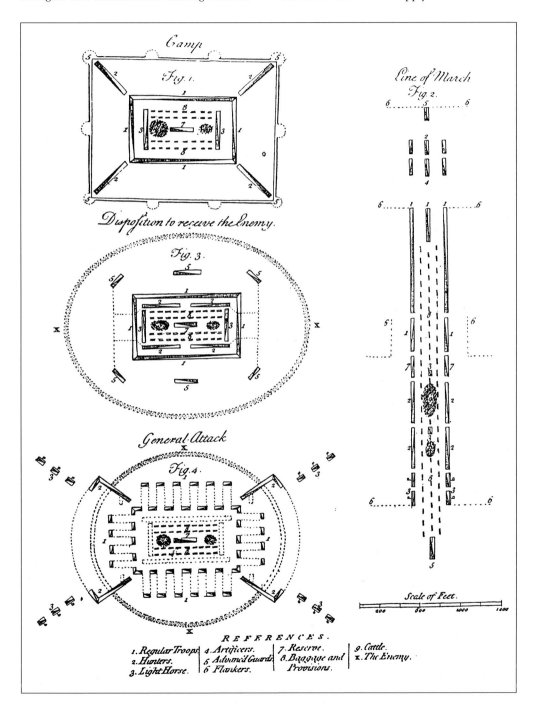

Forest warfare (North America). Compare the line of march in forest conditions to the continental style. The deployment of troops is in sharp contrast to continental linear style.

Prussia

At the beginning of the war, the Prussian army stood at 145,000 men, and was considered the most effective in Europe in linear formation combat. This was achieved by thorough training in the tactics of marching, extending into line and fire control, and the oblique order employed at Leuthen in 1757 was the high-water mark of this very detailed and disciplined system. In analyzing their performance, the Austrian commander Henry Lloyd (who served as an officer in the French,

Prussian Grenadier of the 3rd Battalion, 15th Regiment (Garde). (Osprey Publishing)

Prussian, and Russian armies over the course of 40 years) noted: 'they have a facility in manoeuvring beyond any other troops' (*Annual Register*, 1766). In the period following the War of the Austrian Succession, Frederick had also reformed the heavy cavalry into the best in Europe, and their shock value produced immediate results by inflicting a heavy first blow upon their enemies. Belief in their capabilities promoted a certain level of arrogance in Frederick's army, which was undermined by subsequent Austrian and Russian victories.

The Prussians had a very organized system for maintaining the manpower of their army in the field. A canton system had been introduced in the 1720s and 1730s that regularly called forward all of the able-bodied men in a given district. The best men would proceed to a regular unit for service, and would serve and train with the regular regiment for a year, while the rest would train with a garrison regiment in the area. After the campaign season, the regular troops would return home to farm, and would continue to be called upon, undergoing a retraining session with each recall. The regulars would report first to their regiment in time of war, while the group who had trained with the garrison unit would act as a reserve for the regiment in the field. The Seven Years' War lasted longer than expected, however, and the canton system was inadequate to keep regiments at full strength and adequately trained. The army was slowly being bled white in numbers and quality by 1759.

A second major source of manpower for the Prussian army was foreigners. It is estimated that, by 1756, up to 25 percent of the army was made up of mercenaries, recruited from throughout Europe. As the war progressed, deserters and prisoners from other armies were also pressed into service to increase numbers.

Frederick was innovative in developing horse artillery and the use of howitzers to increase the firepower of both his infantry and cavalry in the field during the war. The major failing of Frederick and his army was their inability to deal with the Austrian light troops, the *Grenzer*. Frederick failed to

British soldier of the 60th Royal American Regiment (North America). Note the hatchet, which was used primarily to fell trees and branches, but also served as an excellent close quarter weapon. (Osprey Publishing)

'sending out patrols of Hussars, to scour the country round the camp' (*Military Instructions for the Generals of his Army*, pp. 3–4).

The Prussian army did survive the war. Its ability to wage war on different fronts and carry victory while sustaining defeat made it the envy of the European armies ranged against it. The Prussian army became the model that many armies emulated after the conflict, not recognizing that it had flaws as well as strengths.

Great Britain

On the eve of war, the British army numbered around 90,000 men. This number would reach close to 150,000 men over the course of the war, but finding enough men for the army was a perennial problem, as was filling the ranks of the Royal Navy and the local militias. Press gangs and prisons were important sources of recruits for both services. Most of the army was deployed overseas in the colonies or at home.

The greatest strength of the British army during the Seven Years' War was its ability to adapt to conditions. When the army was required to wage war in North America, it became clear that traditional linear tactics were not suitable for fighting in the heavily wooded terrain of the frontier. To be effective in the woods, soldiers needed to be lightly armed and mobile. They needed to move quickly, in small groups, as well as in long lines carrying heavy arms and baggage. After a number of reverses, the army began to adopt new tactics better suited to its environment, raising local ranger-style units and employing light infantry trained in skirmishing in the woods.

Formal recognition of this innovation happened in two ways. Two light infantry regiments, the 55th and 80th Foot, were employed in this type of warfare. Additionally, the 60th Royal American Regiment was raised from the frontier populations of North America and from Ireland and England. The intent of the 60th was unique: to combine the forest fighting tactics of the French and their allied

recognize the value of light troops, and thus the Austrians were able to wreak havoc among the Prussian troops, reconnoitering their positions and causing damage in hilly and wooded terrain. Frederick did create units called *Frei-Corps*, whose role was to deal with the Austrian light troops. However, since they were never properly trained or disciplined for this role (being made up of prisoners of war and deserters), the *Frei-Corps* units confined their activities to plunder and pillage in most areas. The regular troops had only contempt for them, and they eventually became cannon fodder for the regular line infantry. Frederick did create a true arm of Hussar cavalry, but he employed them to capture deserters in addition to carrying out their combat duties,

Native Americans with the discipline of a regular soldier. The experiences and tactics of these units were evaluated and conveyed to the rest of the army, and by 1759 regular British army units had eight line companies and one grenadier and one light company. This innovation enabled the British army to match the French in both the woods and the open plains of North America.

The British-allied army in Germany, His Britannic Majesty's Army, was chiefly organized along normal continental lines. British and Hanoverian infantry units won praise at Minden, while the cavalry performed well at Warburg. There was a strong light infantry element, but it was mostly German in origin. The British did not send light troops to Germany until 1760. The German light troops had proved their worth in various skirmishes with the French, and had also provided a wealth of intelligence to their commander.

The British army units serving in India were also trained and fought along continental lines. The officers and men were seconded to the various East India Company forces to stiffen them. The British lagged behind the French in training and organizing their native Sepoy troops along European lines, and this error was not rectified until 1759. The improved battlefield performance of the native troops was witnessed at the Battle of Wandiwash, where the British commander, Colonel Eyre Coote, had two companies of Sepoys as his bodyguard during the battle (Coote's Journal, II, 22/1/60).

Henry Lloyd criticized the British army for the practice of buying and selling commissions. He felt that the purchase system should be abolished, but that with that innovation, combined with better discipline, 'they would surpass any troops in the world' (*Annual Register*, 1766).

Russia

The Russian army's strength was 333,000 men, divided into 174,000 field forces and the rest militia and garrison

troops. During the war, Russia usually only committed between 60,000 and 90,000 men to any one campaign. The vast numerical superiority of the Russian state was the army's greatest asset. After a bloody encounter, the Russians were able to field more reinforcements than Prussia could ever hope to. Reforms had been drawn up to improve the army, but they were only implemented as the war began and did not begin to show results until the end.

The Russian army was perceived as a large, unwieldy, disorganized machine when it marched into battle. This perception was demonstrated in one part of the combined agreements between the Russians and Austrians in 1759, which stated that when the Russians reached the Oder river, the Austrians would take over supplying their provisions. The inadequate supply network had played a role in the Russian generals' planning and prevented them from following up their victory at Kunersdorf in 1759. The campaigns of 1758 and 1759 saw the Russians being forced to pull back from the Oder region to their supply depots in Poland, giving up any land gained. One of the first signs that reforms had begun to take hold was the improvement of the Russian supply train in the later years of the war.

Most observers also had a poor opinion of the Russian general officers. The Russian generals themselves were contemptuous of one another for various reasons, and the general staff was not sufficiently well organized to offset the generals' ineptitude. The Russian armies marched forward in large columns spread over vast areas, and it took a strong commander to bring all the forces together at one time or to follow up a victory. Frederick noted: 'had the Russians known how to profit from victory [Kunersdorf], and pursued the disheartened troops, Prussia would have been ruined beyond redemption' (Frederick II, *History of the Seven Years War*, II, p. 32). At times the number of officers of the low and middle rank was below strength for each regiment, which caused further command and control problems.

The reforms caused organizational disruptions throughout the army. These were

Russian non-commissioned officer from a line regiment. (Osprey Publishing)

by its performance at Zorndorf. It was restructured into more highly organized bodies, enabling it to play a larger role at Kunersdorf, stopping the Prussian advance and inflicting heavy casualties.

Austria

The Austrian army stood at 201,000 men in 1756. The Austrians had set up a reform commission after the defeats of the Silesian Wars in 1748 and, impressed by the discipline and drill of the Prussians, had written drill manuals and distributed them throughout the army. Intensive training was implemented through the formation of new units, which were organized differently to their older counterparts. This caused great difficulty when the units were maneuvering and deploying for battle, but the infantry and artillery benefited greatly in battle, especially defensively. As demonstrated at Zorndorf and Kunersdorf, the Russians were excellent soldiers in defense. An Austrian commander noted: 'their [the Russians'] courage alone has rendered them victorious in spite of all these difficulties in which the general ignorance of their officers involved them' (Lloyd, *Annual Register*, 1766). The artillery wing also underwent a transformation during the war, sparked

Officer of the Austrian Artillery Corps. (Osprey Publishing)

established for all of the various branches. Fire discipline of the regular line infantry was improved, although still not to the same level as that of the Prussians. Prince Joseph Wenzel Liechtenstein, who had been appointed the Director of Artillery in 1744, published a training manual and generally made the artillery more professional, enabling it to play a significant role by applying devastating volleys against the Prussian infantry. The Austrian army changed considerably in eight years, and the British General Joseph Yorke noted that Frederick was 'very far from having contempt for the Austrians but the contrary and I heard him several times call to his officers and bid them to take notice of what the enemy did well in order to learn from it' (Yorke to Earl Hardwicke, 31/7/58).

The Austrian generals were aware of the devastating firepower and maneuverability of the Prussian army – one reason why they adopted a defensive strategy throughout most of the war, preferring to fight among the hills and woods of Bohemia and Silesia. Frederick had a difficult time dealing with the Austrians in hilly fortified positions due to the lack of mobility of his forces.

Another significant reason for this defensive strategy was the Austrians' use of the *Grenzer* corps. These troops, also referred to as *Croates* and *Pandours* by contemporaries, were made up of soldiers from the Balkan frontier regions. This region was a heavily militarized zone, and warfare called for small irregular corps to wage small-scale battles by constant skirmishing. The Austrians used this military corps as light troops, employing them to reconnoiter, forage, and skirmish. They were deployed on the flanks of the army as it marched, and would report on the movements and dispositions of the Prussians before battle. During battle, they would attack the flanks of the Prussian lines, trying to get them to fire and break ranks. The corps numbered 34,000 infantry and 6,000 Hussar cavalry at the beginning of the conflict. Frederick stated: 'the most formidable enemy he has to fight with are the Croats ... who are hardy, brave people faithful to their sovereign ... more on his guard against them than against any other troops ...

it was impossible for him to oppose anything equal to them' (Yorke to Hardwicke, 31/7/58).

Similar to the Russians, the Austrians also suffered from inferior generals. While excellent in defense, the Austrians were often slow to carry out an offensive, largely because their generals failed to launch offensive action in a coordinated fashion. Frederick noted that one of the reasons for his survival was 'the lack of unity between the Russian and Austrian generals, which made them circumspect when the occasion required that they should act with vigour to overwhelm Prussia' (Frederick II, *History of the Seven Years War*, II, p. 268).

France

The Seven Years' War marked the low point for the French army of the eighteenth century. The total force numbered over 200,000 men and suffered from poor high-level leadership, lack of discipline, a lackluster officer class, and delays in implementing necessary reforms. There were, however, some exceptions to the rule among the French forces in the colonies.

The French troops stationed in North America were excellent frontier and linear formation soldiers. The British learned from early defeats at their hands to apply similar tactics to their own training strategies. The French East India Company troops were also of high quality. In the late 1740s they implemented the formal instruction of native troops in linear warfare. The British, as in North America, learned from defeat and applied French theories to their own troops in the region. The French were not able to reinforce their colonial forces after 1758 because the Royal Navy had been successful in denying the French navy access to its own colonies. At the same time, the British heavily reinforced their colonies, outnumbering the French.

Over the course of the war, the decline in discipline among the French army units in North America and India became a factor. At the Plains of Abraham, French troops opened fire too early and lost cohesion after the

British volleys. In India, interruptions in payment of the soldiers' wages led to widespread disruption and desertion in the units of the Company, Regulars, and Marines. The British took advantage of this by signing deserting French soldiers into their forces.

French grenadier and regimental colors. (Osprey Publishing)

The majority of the regular French army was used to wage war against His Britannic Majesty's Army in Germany, and all of its major problems were apparent in the German campaign. As the armies went to war, the French army was undergoing training in new tactics, but these had not had sufficient time to take effect and the French were outclassed by the ability of their opponents to deploy quickly. The tactical and organizational changes began to bear fruit late in the war, but by then it was too late to change the outcome in France's favor. During each campaign the army lost a fifth of its strength to casualties, sickness, and especially desertion. This was a serious problem for the French army in Germany because the pay system collapsed repeatedly and on these occasions the relaxed discipline of the French army became glaringly apparent.

To make matters worse, there was a serious shortage of officers in the field, who were needed to instill discipline and order to units during the campaign season. Henry Lloyd noted of the French army: 'if repulsed their spirits are exhausted so much so that it is difficult for them to attack again … they become mutinous and blame their leaders and desert' (*Annual Register*, 1766). High-level commanders also failed to unite in strength at important times to overwhelm His Britannic Majesty's Army in Germany. Troops from several small German states allied with France and Austria served with the French army in Germany (*Reichsarmee*). However, these small German states did not contribute the same number or quality of soldiers as those serving in His Britannic Majesty's Army. The German troops did not train in peacetime and performed abysmally at Rossbach. They were only fit for garrison and lines of communications duties.

The French army did recognize the value of light troops and the various tactical changes of march and battle order, and these were to be central pieces of the later Napoleonic French armies. However, they were not as successful in their infancy during the Seven Years' War.

The gathering storm

As no single event launched the Seven Years' War, it is simplest to describe the military events of 1756 and relate them to the political events of 1756 and early 1757, when formal war had finally been declared by all states. This chapter focuses on developments in North America, Minorca, and Saxony as the further catalysts for the war.

In North America only one major engagement took place in 1756. The French and the British governments had appointed new commanders-in-chief for their respective campaigns in North America. The French appointed Marquis Louis Joseph de Montcalm, while the British appointed General John Campbell (Earl of Loudon). Montcalm arrived in North America with reinforcements of 1,000 regulars and six ships of the line. The French attacked and destroyed the British fort at Oswego in August. Montcalm then reinforced the French Fort Carillon (Ticonderoga) at the southwestern end of Lake Champlain, after which both sides went into winter quarters as no fighting had erupted in the Lake George region.

The French invasion of Minorca in April 1756 was the event that finally sparked a formal declaration of war between France and Great Britain. The Royal Navy had a major base at Port Mahon on Minorca and another at Gibraltar, and they were under orders to intercept any French movement in the Mediterranean and to observe French preparations in the port of Toulon. There had been reports that the French were preparing an invasion fleet against Great Britain from various bases, and Admiral John Byng was sent to the region with an additional 10 ships of the line to protect the two naval bases. The Royal Navy had already deployed many ships of the line to protect commerce between the West Indies and North America, as well as to intercept any French shipping either dealing in commerce or reinforcement of overseas garrisons. The British had 2,500 troops on the island of Minorca, while the French, under the command of Admiral Count Augustin de la Gallissonniere, had assembled an invasion force of 12 ships of the line and 15,000 soldiers.

The French had landed and invested Port Mahon by the middle part of April. By 8 May they had opened fire on the defenders of Port Mahon, the same day that British reinforcements left Gibraltar. When news of the French invasion reached London, Great Britain acted, formally declaring war on France on 17 May 1756. The naval battle of Minorca occurred on 20 May; Byng's squadron by this time numbered 13 ships of the line. The British had five ships heavily damaged, and the French pulled away and blockaded Port Mahon. Byng felt that the reinforcements he had on board were not sufficient to lift the siege of Port Mahon, and he returned to Gibraltar, forcing the garrison on Minorca to surrender on 28 May. Admiral Byng was later tried by court martial, convicted of not doing his utmost, and shot.

It soon became apparent that the struggle between Great Britain and France was going to engulf the continent of Europe. The need to employ the Royal Navy to protect commerce and impede the French use of the sea-lanes was recognized, and it was suggested that a more aggressive land campaign in the colonies would be necessary. Both Britain and France realized that the war in the colonies was going to be a long fight. France recognized that Hanover was a liability for Britain, and that Britain had difficulties raising new units for the army. The situation reached a critical stage in 1756 when Hanover had to provide troops to Britain to protect her shores from a possible French invasion.

Frederick II of Prussia saw the war clouds gathering on the horizon. He knew from his spies in the capitals of Europe that Austria and

Central Europe

Russia were mobilizing their forces, and in June he began to mobilize his own in response. He thought that the Electorate of Saxony, being wealthy and strategically located, might be involved in the Austrian and Russian preparations. The Prussians had completed their mobilization by the end of August, and on the 29th Frederick crossed into Saxony with 63,000 men. The Saxon army, numbering only 18,000 troops, fell back before the Prussian advance. They retreated to their fortified camp at Pirna, where the Prussians blockaded them. Concluding that the camp was a well-defended location, Frederick decided to starve his opponents out, and his troops occupied Dresden and Leipzig. More troops, under the command of Prince Ferdinand of Brunswick, were sent to the Bohemian border to establish winter quarters. Meanwhile, an Austrian army detachment of 40,000 men, under the command of Marshal Maximilian U. von Browne, was approaching the Prussians on the

Bohemian border, intending to push into
Saxony and lift the siege at Pirna.

Frederick initially sent reinforcements to
Ferdinand, but on 30 September he marched
with 29,000 troops to take personal command
of the situation. His troops assembled near
the plain at Lobositz, and both armies
prepared for battle. The Prussians had
18,000 infantry, 10,500 cavalry, and
97 artillery pieces. The Austrians massed
26,500 infantry, both regular and irregular,
7,500 cavalry, and 94 artillery pieces. As
Frederick approached the Austrian lines,
skirmishing was already taking place on his
left side on Lobosch Hill. At 7.00 am on
1 October he dispatched a cavalry force to
reconnoiter the Austrian lines. They were
repulsed by heavy Austrian fire. As members
of the first charge returned, a second cavalry
charge was put in and it too failed to break
through the Austrian lines. Regular infantry
reinforced the Austrian irregulars on the slope
of Lobosch as a Prussian infantry attack fell
in, and after six hours of fighting the
Prussians were unable to dislodge the
Austrians. A final attack was made against the
Lobosch slope, and this time the Prussians
broke through. The Prussian infantry then
pushed into the town under a heavy artillery
barrage, driving the Austrians back before
them. Both sides had lost equal numbers –
around 3,000 men – but the Prussians had
changed their opinion of Austrian capabilities.
As one soldier noted, 'they're not the same
old Austrians' (Duffy, *Army of Frederick the
Great*, p. 252).

The Austrians had succeeded in sending a
small corps to rescue the Saxons at Pirna,
expecting that their arrival would spur a

Saxon move against the Prussians. Instead,
the Saxon army surrendered on 17 October
1756. Frederick assembled the defeated troops
and announced that they would be
incorporated into the Prussian army –
unusually, as whole units. The general
practice was to break up units and disperse
them among existing regiments, and
Frederick's decision was to have repercussions
in the future, when whole Saxon battalions
would desert the Prussians and switch their
allegiance to either the Austrians or the
French. The British envoy, Sir Andrew
Mitchell, was present when the Prussian
army incorporated the Saxon troops. In a
letter he stated:

*Sunday the 17th the Saxon troops proceeded by
their general officers ... marched into a plain in
the neighbourhood and after passing between two
battalions of Prussian Guards ... had the articles
of war read and the military oath administered to
them ... as every regiment was sworn separately,
this ceremony lasted this and the next day.
(Mitchell to Earl Holdernesse, 21 October 1756)*

The military events of 1756 destroyed any
hope of a peaceful solution to the situation
in Europe. The events in Saxony indicated
that a war on the continent was inevitable
and that Great Britain and France would
have no choice but to be part of it. By
11 January 1757, Russia had become the
third signatory to the First Treaty of
Versailles, sealing the alliance of Russia,
Austria, and France against Prussia and Great
Britain. Great Britain and Prussia meanwhile
began to make their Convention of
Westminster into an offensive arrangement.

World war

Overview of the war

Theaters of operation

The fighting during the war can be divided into distinct theaters of operation. The naval conflict was chiefly between the British and the French, as were the conflicts in North America and the Caribbean. On the North American frontier, the British suffered early defeats because the army was not properly trained or equipped to fight in wooded terrain. By 1758 these deficits had been remedied and the tide had turned in favor of the British. In 1760 the British launched a three-pronged attack against the last remnants of the French in North America, and by the end of the year they had achieved their aim of destroying the French presence in North America.

The western European theater of operations was in western Germany, between the French and the British-allied German armies. After initial defeats, the British-allied army rallied to protect the western flank of Prussia and secure Hanover against French occupation.

The central European theater of operations was the scene of the battles and campaigns of the Prussians, Austrians, and Russians. Most of the fighting occurred in Saxony, Silesia, Bohemia, and the Oder River region. Frederick began the war with the intent of striking against and occupying the wealthy province of Saxony. His strategy of 1757 was to deliver a knockout blow against the main Austrian army before the Russians had fully entered the war, and that year was marked by a series of major battles that nevertheless failed to deliver the vital victory that Frederick had wished for. His revised strategy in 1758 was to deliver attacks upon the Austrians and Russians that would prevent them from forming a united front, but his losses mounted and in 1759 his strategy changed radically, to one of strategic defense. His plan was to allow his enemies both to come against him and then to exploit the advantage of interior lines to defeat first one and then the other. He had selected this plan when he recognized that the Austrians and Russians were proving difficult to defeat when fighting on the defensive. The rest of the war was spent attempting to stop the Austrians and Russians uniting and destroying the main Prussian corps in the field.

The last theater of operations to be considered was on the Indian subcontinent. Chiefly, this was a war between two commercial enterprises, the French and English East India Companies. The war was on a small scale compared to the battles of Europe and North America, but the prize of dominance in India was nevertheless an important one. Both companies deployed locally raised troops, both native and European, reinforced by a sprinkling of regular troops provided by their respective governments. The campaigns began in Bengal in 1756 and were concluded in Britain's favor in 1757 after the Battle of Plassey. The conflict then switched to a southern region, the Carnatic, where the war took on a more European flavor. The French were first on the offensive in 1758, but were unable to hold the advantage for long due to reverses in the naval situation. British success in blockading the French navy meant that the French were effectively cut off from any hope of reinforcements by sea.

The naval war

The naval war was chiefly fought between Britain and France. The Royal Navy had a tonnage of 277,000 tons in 1755 and 375,000 tons in 1760. The French navy had 162,000 tons in 1755 and 156,000 tons in 1760. The British had feared that the French and Spanish would join in an alliance, because the combined force of the two nations would have exceeded that of the Royal Navy. In the event, Spain did not join the war until 1762, after the French had been swept from the seas, leaving Britain free to concentrate on this new naval opponent.

The Royal Navy engaged in three different forms of strategy during the war. The first was the seizure and destruction of the French trading fleet across the world's oceans, which

HMS *George* (right, first rate) alongside the launching of HMS *Cambridge* (third rate) in 1757. (National Maritime Museum)

denied the French government a large percentage of the revenue raised from the colonies and had the added benefit of increasing British revenue for the war effort. The second was the tying up and emasculating of the French fleet by blockade in its home waters. The third and final strategy was the combined operations role of the fleet in carrying the war to the colonies and France. This last role is dealt with later in the book. During the war, the Royal Navy was able to increase its numbers of ships both by construction and by seizure of French (and later Spanish) fighting ships. The Royal Navy

built or captured 69 ships, whereas the combined French and Spanish navies only added a total of six ships to their fleets. The French navy's biggest problem was a lack of unified strategy at the government level, since opinion at the French court was divided between those who favored concentrating on naval and colonial warfare, and those who favored a war in Europe and felt that a naval war was secondary to the seizure of Hanover.

The naval term 'ship of the line' refers to three-masted, square-rigged vessels with 60 or more cannon on board (i.e. the minimum firepower to be able to stand in the line of

battle against an enemy). Ships with fewer than 60 cannon were referred to as cruisers and frigates. First rate ships carried 90–100 or more guns; second rate usually fielded 80–90 guns; third rate ships had 64–74 guns. Fourth rate ships (frigates) usually carried 50 guns. Fifth and sixth rate ships (cruisers) carried 24–40 guns. Each navy attempted to standardize its own ratings, but captured foreign ships and changes in design made this difficult. The Royal Navy return for 10 April 1759 lists the following: two ships of the first rating, 10 of the second rating, 40 of the third, 47 of the fourth, 32 of the fifth, and 60 of the sixth (Hardwicke Papers 35898).

Naval tactics in use at this time had been developed during the previous century. The most commonly used tactic was called line-ahead, which was similar to the linear formations of the land armies. The idea was for a squadron to form in line and attack the enemy fleet with a broadside fire along a continuous line. The ships would give covering fire to each other as they progressed down the line of the enemy. However, some admirals hoped for a melee or penetration of the enemy's line of ships, because otherwise battles could easily descend into ship-versus-ship engagements. Another advantage of the melee was that the line-ahead formation could be broken at a critical moment in battle to destroy fleeing enemy ships or penetrating ships. Royal Navy commanders had been given 'Fighting Instructions' that tied them rigidly to the line-ahead tactics. However, at various times commanders changed tactics and employed the melee. In the early part of the war, superior French shipbuilding gave them more maneuverability and thus a strategic advantage. By 1756 the British had recognized this and had begun to improve their own designs. They also examined and impressed any captured French ships into British service as soon as they were taken.

The Royal Navy deployed the majority of its fleet in the North American theater and in home waters, intending to disrupt the lucrative trade between France and her colonies as well as to protect Great Britain from a possible French invasion. The French

accounted for about 10 percent of British commercial shipping.

The Royal Navy suffered reverses in 1757 and 1758 in the coastal expeditions against Rochefort and St Malo, and in the Louisbourg campaign of 1757. However, in 1758 the British Admiral Henry Osborne defeated a French force in Spanish waters attempting to relieve pressure on the Toulon fleet. The British Admiral Sir Edward Hawke defeated a French force near Basque Roads, which was preparing to sail to New France. The French inability to unite their Toulon, Brest, and Le Havre fleets to overwhelm the Royal Navy blockade was to be a decisive factor in these victories; the Royal Navy had the advantage in 1758 of bases such as Gibraltar close at hand, which enabled it to mask the Toulon base and develop new resupply methods for the fleet off Brest. The British also improved the port of Halifax in Nova Scotia, and this proved decisive in the campaigns against Louisbourg and Quebec. After the fall of the French naval base at Louisbourg in 1758, the Royal Navy could sail into the St Lawrence region at least a month earlier from Halifax and Louisbourg than if it had sailed from Great Britain. Only the break-up of the ice floes impeded its progress.

The year 1759 was marked by two decisive engagements that ended French naval attempts to gain a decisive advantage. The French Commodore, the Marquis de la Clue, sailed with 12 ships of the line from Toulon for Brest. The British Admiral Edward Boscawen, commander at Gibraltar, with 14 ships of the line, sailed to intercept the French. On 18 August the two fleets met off the Portuguese coast at Lagos. The British captured three ships and destroyed two others. The French withdrew and sailed for Lisbon, where the British blockaded them.

Even after the loss at Lagos, the French continued to prepare for an invasion of Britain to offset pressure on New France. In November 1759, a major part of the Royal Navy blockading force off Brest returned to port at Torbay due to a storm. The French decided to seize this moment and launch a naval attack. The French Admiral Hubert

Admiral Edward Boscawen, victor of Louisbourg in 1758 and Lagos Bay in 1759. (National Maritime Museum)

navy was initially successful at the outbreak of war; it seized Minorca and reinforced New France. In 1757 the Royal Navy began to intercept French shipping in the Gulf of Mexico and seized a large quantity of prizes. They also began to blockade the major French ports in an attempt to seize or destroy French naval units, and seized neutral shipping, using the claim that the cargo was intended for the French market. The British government also hired privateers to search and seize French and neutral shipping. This policy upset many neutral states, but they were powerless to oppose it. British commercial shipping by 1758 had a naval protection force (convoy) to offset any French naval attacks, although French privateering efforts eventually de Conflans sailed with 21 ships of the line and supporting frigates, and encountered some of the remaining Royal Navy ships. The British Admiral Edward Hawke shortly caught up with the French force, leading 25 ships of the line, plus various supporting cruisers and frigates. The French withdrew towards Quiberon Bay, hoping its natural defense of reefs would prevent the Royal Navy squadron from pursuing. The Royal Navy followed despite the dangers of rocks and reefs and on 20 November battle ensued. Hawke destroyed or captured seven ships while losing only two of his own, and the French withdrew further after being scattered. This was the last major French attempt to invade the British Isles; most of the French fleet remained in port for the rest of the war.

The Royal Navy continued to patrol off the various French bases. It also increased pressure on the French commercial fleets throughout the world. In 1760 France, due to the losses in New France and to her commercial fleet, had problems funding her war effort in Germany and paying the annual subsidy to Austria. The Royal Navy, with other areas secure, sought a more aggressive combined operations policy in the Caribbean against the French and, by 1762, the Spanish colonies.

1757

North America
Lord Loudon waited through the first months of 1757 for specific instructions for the campaign in North America. In April he was directed to attack the French naval port of Louisbourg on Cape Breton Island. Louisbourg was a well-garrisoned and important base for the French navy. It also protected the entry to the St Lawrence River basin, which was the central route of trade for New France. Loudon was forced to withdraw many of his regular troops from the New York frontier to gather sufficient strength for the attack. By early July the British had assembled seven battalions of

regulars in Halifax, where they awaited the naval squadron that would carry the force and engage any French naval units at Louisbourg. However, while they were waiting, news arrived that the French had 22 ships of the line at Louisbourg as well as 7,000 men. This force was thought to be too large to engage and the decision was made to cancel the expedition and return the troops to New York.

In the meantime, the French had seized the opportunity offered when the New York frontier was stripped of so many British regulars. Montcalm had assembled 8,000 French, Canadian militia, and allied Native Americans at the northern end of Lake George, dividing his force into two, with 2,500 men marching overland and 5,000 men in whale boats sailing down the lake. Their object was the British Fort William Henry, commanded by Lieutenant-Colonel Munro, on the southern end of the lake. By 3 August the French had surrounded the fort and begun to lay siege, and within three days they had opened fire on the western side of the fort with artillery.

The fort was equipped with 17 guns and 2,200 men, a mix of regulars and provincials, and was sorely in need of reinforcement at this point. The closest fort, Fort Edward, lay 14 miles (22km) south of Fort William Henry. Its British commander, Colonel Webb, was waiting for reinforcements to arrive before moving out. He had collected a force of 4,000 men, regulars and provincials, but having received intelligence that Montcalm had 12,000 men, felt that he needed still more troops. Webb sent a letter to Fort William Henry advising the British to seek terms of surrender, and the letter was intercepted by Montcalm's troops. They increased the pressure on the fort, and on 9 August Munro capitulated, having lost more than 300 of his men. The British were allowed to leave with their regimental colors, armed for their safety against native attacks, and to be escorted by a French regiment to Fort Edward. On the way, a force of French-allied Native Americans estimated at 3,000 attacked the

British column. French regulars tried to stop the native attacks, but more than 100 people were killed during the attack, women and children among them.

This engagement effectively destroyed the British presence on Lake George. The French burned the fort and returned to Fort Carillon (Ticonderoga) in the north, and both sides rested and began to prepare for the campaign of 1758. Skirmishing on the frontier between the British and French,

and the Native Americans allied with each side, continued.

Western Europe

After Frederick's move into Saxony, France was obliged to honor her agreement to provide 24,000 troops to the Austrian cause, and accordingly began to prepare for an invasion of Hanover and the Prussian provinces of Geldern and Cleve. Frederick II notified the British envoy, Sir Andrew

Battle of Quiberon Bay, 20 November 1759 – detail of ships breaking up in the foreground.
(National Maritime Museum)

to provide an additional 8,000–10,000 men, and to ask the states of Brunswick and Saxe-Gotha to provide a further 10,000 men. The troops from Hesse, Brunswick, and Saxe-Gotha would be paid for by a British subsidy, and the Hanoverians owed allegiance to the King of England since he was also the Elector of Hanover. The British Cabinet agreed to Frederick's plan for an 'Army of Observation' (Allied army), paid for with British money but employing no British troops, to protect Hanover and the Prussian provinces in the west against France.

By March 1757, French troops were on the move. The army was estimated at 100,000 men, which included Austrian and German-allied troops. The army was commanded first by Lieutenant-General Prince Soubise, and later (from 27 April) by Marshal d'Estrées. The Allied army numbered only 47,000 men, of which a large Hanoverian contingent had not yet arrived from England. On 30 March the Duke of Cumberland, son of George II, was given command of the Allied army, under orders to protect the dominions of Prussia and Hanover but not to act offensively. In early April the French crossed the Rhine and advanced towards Wesel, and on 1 May the Second Treaty of Versailles was signed. This was an offensive agreement among France, Austria, and Russia that called for France to provide 105,000 troops and to subsidize 10,000 German troops for the war against Prussia. France was also to provide 22.5 million livres to Austria for her war effort. The aims of the signatories were to destroy Prussia's military potential and to support Austria's claim to Silesia.

The French continued to advance against the Allied army, and in early June Cumberland decided to stop and fight at Brackwede. However, Soubise was able to send his light troops around the flanks of the Allies and threaten their communications, and Cumberland decided to withdraw. The

Mitchell, of the French intentions, and estimated that the French were gathering an army of 50,000 men. The British did not wish to send forces to the region; recruitment was problematic and the government considered the war in the colonies its first priority. Frederick suggested a plan for the Hessian and Hanoverian troops stationed in Britain to return to Hanover to protect the region in the event of an invasion. Since this would amount to only 35,000 men, Prussia offered

French continued to advance on the heels of the Allies and to outmaneuver them. Finally, on 24 July Cumberland began to dig emplacements in the Hastenbeck and Voremberg areas. Skirmishing between forward units began, with both sides trying to gain intelligence to identify the intentions of the enemy.

Soubise recognized that Cumberland was digging in for battle. The two sides stood as follows: the French army had 50,000 infantry, 10,000 cavalry, and 68 guns, while the Allied army had 30,000 infantry, 5,000 cavalry, and 28 guns. Cumberland's main line of infantry was to be drawn north of Hastenbeck and along the road running east. The left and center positions of his line were heavily defended, but his right wing did not require much protection, naturally defended as it was by marshy fields.

The French attack was aimed at the center of Cumberland's line, with an attack against Obensburg. The French knew they had superiority in numbers of artillery and men, marching against the hill feature of Obensburg, which was protected by three companies of jaegers. At 3.00 am on 26 July

Battle of Prague, 6 May 1757.
(National Army Museum, Chelsea)

the French advance began, and by 8.00 am
the entire line was marching against its
Allied counterparts. The battlefield shortly
became so confused that both sides fired
upon their own men in the melee. Both
commanders were given incorrect reports of
attacks on the flanks and other positions.
D'Estrées saw his own cavalry moving from
one side of the front to the other when he
had given no such order. Upon receiving
further intelligence of Allied movements, he
ordered his troops to withdraw from the field
at about 2.00 pm. Reaching the south side of
the Haste River, he received reports that
Cumberland too had withdrawn from the

field of battle. This proved to be the case:
Cumberland was in full retreat and d'Estrées
sent his units back across the Haste to take
the field of battle and follow up the
enemy. The French lost 1,000 killed and
1,200 wounded, and the Allies 311 killed,
900 wounded, and 200 missing.

Following this battle, most of Hanover
was occupied by the French army. On
8 September Cumberland signed the
Convention of Kloster Zeven with the
French. This stipulated that the Hanoverian
Allied army was to be demobilized and that
prisoners of war were to be exchanged.

The British government believed that, if
the Royal Navy and army were deployed in
combined operations against the coast of
France, the French army would need to
redeploy forces from the Hanover front to
the French coastal regions. The British
government still did not want to send British
troops to Hanover, fearing that they would be
tied down in the region for many months.

Ten regiments were assembled on the Isle
of Wight with the intention of attacking the
French port of Rochefort. The troops spent
most of the summer waiting for transports to
arrive. The ships finally put to sea on
8 September, the same day that Cumberland
signed the Convention with the French. By
23 September the fleet and the army had
battered and captured the Isle d'Aix.
However, due to inclement weather and
reports of sizable French reinforcements in
Rochefort, the fleet and army decided against
further action and returned to Portsmouth
on 3 October. Many British raids were made
on the French coast and ports in the
following years of the war.

Central Europe

Frederick II opened the 1757 campaigning
season on 18 April. He invaded Bohemia,
intending a decisive campaign ending with
the destruction of the Austrian army and its
ability to wage war. His Prussians attacked
with four separate corps totaling
116,000 men, who pushed into Bohemia,
converging on a similar axis and hoping to
outmaneuver the Austrians. The Austrian

Western Europe

army was under the dual command of Field Marshal Browne and Prince Charles of Lorraine, brother-in-law of Maria Theresa. Elements of the two armies met on a plateau to the east of Prague in early May. The Prussians amassed 47,000 infantry, 17,000 cavalry, and 210 pieces of artillery, while the Austrians massed 45,000 regular infantry, 2,000 irregulars, 12,600 cavalry, and 60 pieces of artillery.

At 6.00 am on 6 May the two armies engaged. The Austrians had occupied the high ground, and their northern section was also covered by the fortifications of Prague. The Prussians realized after a reconnaissance that the southern area was the probable site for

operations. The Prussian cavalry led the charge in an attempt to roll up the right of the Austrians, and the Austrian horse placed on the right wing scattered. Field Marshal Browne began to reinforce the eastern edge of the plateau with infantry and artillery, while the Prussian first line marched towards the Austrians at the edge of the plateau, only to be driven back by heavy fire. This counter-attack did, however, offer an opportunity to the Prussians: in moving their infantry to the southeast, the Austrians had left a gap in the line to the north. Twenty-two Prussian battalions stormed into the gap to isolate the right wing of the Austrian army from the rest, and then rolled up the Austrians from the left,

Austrian Marshal Leopold J. v. Daun. (Anne S. K. Brown Military Collection, Brown University Library)

successfully pushing them back towards Prague. The Prussians were victorious in this engagement, but they suffered more casualties, losing 14,200 men while the Austrians lost 13,400.

The troops retreated from the battlefield to the gates of Prague. Their numbers, combined with those of the garrison, meant that there were 50,000 Austrian troops in the city. By 29 May Frederick had begun to lay siege to the city with artillery bombardments. If the city had fallen, Frederick could have imposed heavy terms on the Austrians to end the conflict. However, the Austrian Marshal Leopold J. v. Daun had assembled an army in eastern Bohemia consisting of 30,000 men from other regions, along with remnants from the Battle of Prague. Frederick dispatched a force of 18,000 men under the command of Lieutenant-General the Duke of Bevern to offset any moves by Daun, and followed him with an additional 14,000 men, intending to dislodge Daun from his position near Kolin. Daun had been further reinforced in early June and had positioned his men along a low ridge of hills that the Austrians knew well from previous prewar maneuvering exercises.

The Prussians had 19,500 infantry, 15,000 cavalry, and 98 pieces of artillery. The Austrians had amassed 35,000 infantry, 18,000 cavalry, and 154 pieces of artillery. On the night of 17–18 June, the Prussians marched around the Austrian positions, hoping to come up on the ridge behind them and force them onto the plain. The Prussians intended to attack on the flanks of the Austrian right, but were forced to cancel this plan when they emerged from the village of Krzeczor and realized that Daun had anticipated this move and had reinforced toward the east. By mid-afternoon on 18 June, the Prussians had launched a frontal attack against the ridge positions. An Austrian account recalls: 'They [the Prussians] attacked this flank with vivacity at the very moment that the Austrians came up to form it. Despite this, the Austrians repulsed the assault by an intense fire of musketry and artillery' (St Paul, *1757: The Defence of Prague*, p. 151).

After three hours of fighting, the center of the Austrian line began to falter. As the Austrian infantry pushed forward, they once again allowed a gap to develop in the line and the Prussians attempted to capitalize on this. This time, however, Austrian artillery battered the Prussian infantry attempting to force the gap, and the Saxon cavalry charged the Prussian line, inflicting heavy damage. The Austrians ended the battle by seizing the village of Krzeczor, the area of the heaviest fighting throughout the day. An Austrian staff officer noted:

The enemy were entirely routed: some ran on the road towards Kolin – these were captured; others took the road towards Nimburg; a third part went towards Bomimisch-Brod. Thus, as the sun set ending the day, so too ended this glorious battle, which will for ever immortalise the name of Daun. (St Paul, 1757: The Defence of Prague, p. 163)

The British envoy to the Prussians, Sir Andrew Mitchell, wrote a letter to London about the Battle of Kolin which noted that: 'the Prussians attacked with great bravery and intrepidity ... However, the Austrian Army was most advantageously posted' (Mitchell at camp outside Prague, 20 June 1757). The Prussians lost 13,700 men and the Austrians 9,000. With the defeat at Kolin, Frederick was forced to withdraw from Prague and leave Bohemia, enabling the Austrians to amass close to 100,000 men.

The next major battle occurred in East Prussia between the Prussians and the Russians. Due to the Prussian attack on Saxony, the Elector of Saxony and King of Poland gave permission for the Russian army to advance over his territory to strike at Prussia.

The Russians were moving against the East Prussian province by the end of June. East Prussia, isolated from the main Prussian province of Brandenburg/Pomerania, had at its disposal only 32,000 troops under the command of Field Marshal Hans v. Lehwaldt. The Russians, under the overall command of Field Marshal Stephen Fedorovich Apraksin, deployed 55,000 men in five corps along a broad front. They captured the port of Memel on 5 July, and pressed on, intending to march on the East Prussian capital of Königsberg. Lehwaldt decided to attack the Russian columns when they came within striking distance, even though the Prussians, with only 24,000 men, were outnumbered two to one.

On 30 August Lehwaldt and the Prussian army emerged from the west near the town of Gross-Jägersdorf and attacked the Russians at around 5.00 am. The Prussians were spread thinly in linear formation. They had surprised the Russians on the march and tried to take advantage of the ensuing confusion. Heavy fighting took place in the center lines in the Norkitten Wood, but the Russian artillery took a heavy toll of the Prussians. After four salvoes against the center, the Prussian effort was spent and a general retreat began. The Prussians lost 4,500 men and the Russians lost 6,000. The Russians did not follow up the Prussian retreat, allowing them to leave the battlefield without much molestation. The Prussians, for their part, had a newfound respect for the fighting capabilities of the Russians that was reinforced in the later battles of Zorndorf and Kunersdorf.

The Russians decided to withdraw from East Prussia and returned to Poland in October. The reasons for this decision are not clear, but Apraksin was removed from his post as a result and ordered to appear at court in St Petersburg. The Prussian field army also left East Prussia, withdrawing to Pomerania to deal with Swedish attempts to seize territory. The Russians returned to East Prussia in January 1758 with 72,000 men and attacked during the winter snows. The Prussians, without the East Prussian field army, offered no real resistance on this occasion, and the Russians took possession of the province, a position they held until the end of the war. As other battles demonstrate, territorial victories were not as important as destroying the field armies of the enemy.

The next significant engagement was between the Prussians and the French and their German allies (*Reichsarmee*) at Rossbach. This was the only time that the

Prussian field army and the French met during the war. Marshal Soubise led a joint French and *Reichsarmee* of 42,000 men against Brandenburg. After leaving 30,000 troops in the Saxon/Silesia region to hold the Austrian advance and after suffering losses at Kolin, Frederick had 21,000 men at his disposal against the French. After pulling back into central Prussia to rest, Frederick did an about-face as the French began to march east, and by 4 November he was facing the French army near Rossbach. The French and the *Reichsarmee* marched towards the Prussian camp, hoping the Prussians would leave the area. The French were hesitant at first in their approach to the Prussians. When news arrived that the Franco-German

Battle of Leuthen, 5 December 1757. A and M) Prussians send an advance guard as a feint attack. Prussian units wheel around to the right of the Austrian lines. A cavalry force is stationed to protect the flanking movement. B and C) Prussians begin the flank attack on the Austrian left wing. G and H) Austrians form a new line in the town of Leuthen. (Christchurch Library)

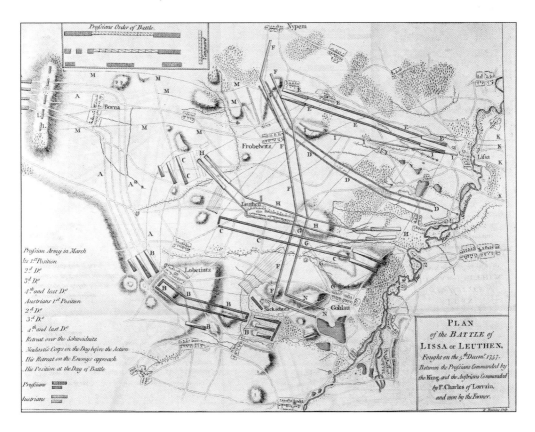

army was on the move, Frederick ordered Major-General Frederick Wilhelm v. Seydlitz to charge the French with 38 squadrons of cavalry. His squadrons smashed into the advance guard of the Franco-Germans and dispersed them easily while the army was still in marching columns. The Prussian infantry followed quickly behind, and the Franco-German infantry rapidly fell into disorder under the onslaught. A contemporary account notes that 'the infantry both French and Imperialists made but a feint resistance' (*Annual Register*, 1762). The Prussian cavalry reformed for a second attack and swept behind the Franco-German infantry, while the Prussian artillery began to take a heavy toll of the Franco-Germans as well. Frederick noted that the battle

Battle of Rossbach, 4 November 1757. (Anne S. K. Brown Military Collection, Brown University Library)

happened so quickly that there was no time for all of his army to get involved and that 'ten battalions of the right had remained ideal spectators' (Frederick II, *History of the Seven Years War*, I, p. 184). The Franco-Germans lost 10,000 men, while the Prussians lost 548.

Frederick had gained a major victory, but he had to turn east immediately to counter a major Austrian attack. The rest of the war was characterized by a system of fighting on interior lines, hitting one army, and then quickly turning to destroy another force. The French did not invade the major Prussian territories again as their campaign from then on was directed against Hanover.

The Austrians had pushed into Silesia by early November, where they were able to defeat a Prussian army of 19,000 before Breslau, the capital of Silesia, on 22 November, and capture the city itself on

25 November. Frederick, with 30,000 troops, moved quickly towards Breslau. He was reinforced by remnants of the defeated Silesian force, which raised the total number to 33,000 men. The Austrians, under the command of Prince Charles of Lorraine, had 66,000 troops. On 5 December, the two armies met at Leuthen. This battle is considered the most brilliant battle conducted by Frederick in his career, and employed the tactic known as the oblique order. Frederick admitted that he wished 'to avoid faults similar to those committed at the Battle of Prague and which caused the loss of the Battle of Kolin' (Frederick II, *History of the Seven Years War*, II, p. 202). The tactic was a most difficult exercise, and was not demonstrated again with the same expertise by the Prussians.

The Austrians deployed in a large open field with almost endless lines of infantry.

Prussian Major-General Frederick Wilhelm v. Seydlitz. (Anne S. K. Brown Military Collection, Brown University Library)

Charles thought that the Prussians would advance and hit the right center of his line, and when the Prussians moved forward at 8.00 am, he reinforced this area. However, Frederick instead sent most of his army to the south under the cover of the ground, shielded from the view of the Austrians. His attack was intended to hit the southern left flank of the Austrians from the side and roll them from the south to the north, causing confusion. He sent a Prussian feint attack into the center of the Austrian line, but the Austrian commander of the left flank, General Nadasti, realized that the Prussians were coming in on his flank and that he needed reinforcements. The Prussians smashed into 14 battalions of Württemburgers and began to push the line north. Charles, realizing the danger, immediately ordered infantry reinforcements to the south, but this

last-minute deployment created a bottleneck in the village of Leuthen. Frederick noted that 'the Austrian guards seeing themselves turned and taken in the flank, endeavoured to change their position; endeavoured too late, to form a parallel to the Prussian front' (Frederick II, *History of the Seven Years War*, I, p. 202).

Prussian artillery and musketry began to take a heavy toll on the Austrians, who by 3.30 pm were retreating from the village of Leuthen. An Austrian cavalry charge was ordered against the Prussian infantry left flank, but they in turn were taken in their flank by Prussian cavalry. The fighting lasted into the evening as the Prussians continued to push north. The Austrians lost 22,000 men, while the Prussians lost 11,000, and Prince Charles was relieved of command for future operations.

Many observers felt that the victory at Leuthen was even greater than that at Rossbach, since the Austrians were viewed as a more professional army than the Franco-Germans. A Prussian witness noted that the 'Austrians defended themselves with great bravery but at last [were] forced to give way ... the enemy's army ... never fought with more bravery than this time' (Lloyd, *History of the Late War in Germany*, I, p. 130). The oblique order was chiefly successful because the Austrians did not identify the threat, largely due to the absence of the Austrian *Grenzer* corps at Leuthen.

Indian subcontinent

The French and English (British) East India Companies had set up their own military organizations, chiefly to protect the various trading posts throughout the region. Both companies had also created alliances with local princes with a view to supplementing company troops with local manpower in the event of war.

The outbreak of hostilities began in the Bengal region in 1756. The British at Calcutta had heard rumors that a war was imminent with France, and the French and British companies in Bengal began to reinforce their stations. The local Nawab, Siraj-ud-daula, disliked the British presence. The British had harbored a rival for his throne in Madras, which had not improved relations. He ordered preparations for war to cease. The French complied but the British continued, so the Nawab moved against the offending stations in Bengal. By the end of June 1756, the Nawab's army had seized all of the British stations, including Calcutta. In the course of taking control, the Nawab's troops herded some 50 or 60 British traders into the small prison at Fort William. The prison was not suitable for the numbers incarcerated there, and close to 40 people died from heat exhaustion caused by the poor ventilation. Although not deliberate, this episode went down in history as the infamous Black Hole of Calcutta. It became a rallying call to defeat the Nawab and avenge the deaths.

The English East India Company dispatched a force of men from Madras to Bengal to take back the various stations. Four ships of the line were assembled under the command of Admiral Charles Watson, carrying 600 European Company troops, three companies of the 39th Foot and 900 Sepoys (Indian Company troops). The troops were all under the overall command of Robert Clive, who had earlier won fame as a military commander of the company's troops during the Second Carnatic War of 1751–53. The fleet and army force easily

Following this victory, the initiative rested with the Prussians for the following year. However, the Prussian army had suffered many casualties in the previous campaigns and had to build up its regiments to acceptable levels, and this influenced future operations. The ability to fight a battle such as Leuthen required a highly trained and disciplined army to move with precision, and many veterans with years of experience had died or been wounded. The Prussians had a difficult time winning subsequent battles, for the Austrians had learned that fighting in an open plain such as Leuthen favored the Prussians. The Austrians also learned to offset the oblique order with better reconnaissance.

seized Calcutta on 30 December 1756, and then moved north to seize Hooghly. This accomplished, they pulled back to Calcutta, where news arrived in mid-January 1757 that war had formally been declared between France and Great Britain.

The Nawab, angered by the attack at Hooghly, moved south towards the British with 40,000 troops. The British, fearing a joint French/Nawab attack on Calcutta, waited to negotiate with the Nawab, which the Nawab did not wish to do. On 4 February a battle broke out between the two forces. The Nawab had 40,000 men, while the British had 600 sailors, 650 European troops, and 800 Sepoys. Clive's attack upon the camp of the Nawab was not very successful; he lost 100 Europeans and 50 Sepoys were killed. The Nawab, however, lost 600 men, and concluded a treaty with the British five days later. As a consequence, the Nawab was forced to return all of the property taken at Calcutta and to reinstate all the privileges granted the British traders in Bengal. Clive then marched to attack the French station of Chandernagore, and received its surrender on 23 March.

The Nawab, fearing the growing threat of the British presence in Bengal, began corresponding with the French East India Company in Pondicherry and Arcot. Unknown to him, however, a conspiracy was brewing in his own household. The Nawab's uncle and paymaster of his army, Mir Jaffar, was the chief conspirator. Clive decided to back Mir Jaffar and, as the Nawab withdrew his army north to Plassey, the conspirators signed a treaty granting Mir Jaffar the throne of Bengal, Orissa, and Bihar in exchange for the transfer of all the French stations in the area to British control.

Clive next decided to attack the Nawab's army at Plassey, nearly 800 miles (1,300km) north of Calcutta. He had 900 European troops, 200 Topasses (native Portuguese soldiers), and 2,100 Sepoys. The British arrived via river transport and overland march to the plain south of Plassey, and on 23 June battle was joined. The Nawab's army numbered 35,000 infantry and 18,000 cavalry, plus a contingent of French artillery from the station at Chandernagore. The British deployed in linear formation, placing European troops in the center and Sepoys and Topasses on the flanks. The French opened the action at 8.00 am with artillery fire, beginning an artillery duel that continued until 11.00 am. A rainstorm drenched the Nawab's powder supply, and the units that he sent to hit the British were dispersed by continuous artillery fire.

Following these setbacks, the Nawab's army began to pull back, and the British launched an attack to gain a good fire position over the enemy. After seizing the water tank area, the Nawab's troops came forward again and were hit by heavy artillery and musket fire. Clive then realized that his flank was covered by troops loyal to Mir Jaffar. He decided on a final push and seized the last of the redoubts and hillock. The Nawab's troops fell back, and by 5.00 pm the battle was over. The following is a statement by an officer of the English East India Company army:

Nawab's army outnumbered the British 20 to 1 but the British had courage, military discipline and what was superior to both was the treachery of the Nawab's officers [Mir Jaffar] … [Clive] obtained a victory, great in consequences but laughable in the act and had not most of the runaways been on foot, it might had been called … the battle of the spurs. (Mss Eur B248)

The British lost 25 men killed and 50 men wounded, while the Nawab is estimated to have lost 500 men. The Nawab escaped the battlefield, only to be murdered after being captured. Mir Jaffar was given the throne of Bengal and the ties established by this alliance with the British made the area a source of revenue in the conflict with the French which followed in the Carnatic area of operations. Although it was an important victory, however, Plassey did not mark the beginning of British domination of the Indian subcontinent, as some sources have claimed. Only the later Battle of Wandiwash and the siege of Pondicherry would secure the British political position.

1758

North America

The British began the campaign season in North America heavily reinforced with both regular and locally raised provincial troops, and planned a three-pronged attack on French territories. The targets were first Fort Carillon (Ticonderoga to the British), on the southwestern end of Lake Champlain, then the fort and port of Louisbourg, the assault on which had originally been intended to take place in 1757. Fort Duquesne, in western Pennsylvania, was the final target.

The French General Montcalm was stationed at Fort Carillon with 4,000 men. The new British commander in North America, General James Abercromby, assembled 7,000 regulars and 9,000 provincial troops at Fort Edward, and on 5 July the whole force sailed north on Lake George. By noon on the 6th, the troops had disembarked at the northern end of the lake and begun marching towards Fort Carillon. The French

had received intelligence that the British were on the move and had called in a reinforcement of 400 regular soldiers, which arrived at Fort Carillon on 4 July. Trees had been felled along the fort's edge to offer better fire spaces and to impede the attackers, and the French also built a large outer trench with more felled trees in front. Montcalm placed seven of his eight regular battalions in the outer defences.

On 8 July the British sent in an attack without artillery support on the strength of intelligence sent to Abercromby, which recommended an immediate attack while the artillery was still some miles back. The provincials attacked in the first wave and were easily repulsed. Abercromby then committed his regular troops, who were held up by the felled trees and raked by French musketry and artillery fire. The British attempted six frontal attacks between 1.00 pm and 6.00 pm, all of which failed. A final attack by the 42nd Highlanders (Black Watch) and the 4th Battalion, 60th Foot Royal American

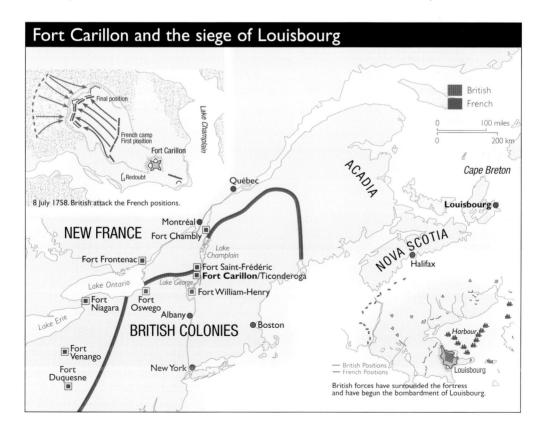

Fort Carillon and the siege of Louisbourg

British

French

0   100 miles

0   200 km

Lake Champlain

Final position

French camp
First position

Fort Carillon

Redoubt

Québec

ACADIA

Cape Breton

Louisbourg

8 July 1758. British attack the French positions.

Montréal

NEW FRANCE   Fort Chambly

Fort Frontenac

Lake Ontario

Fort Niagara

Fort Oswego

Albany

Lake Erie

Lake Champlain

Fort Saint-Frédéric
Fort Carillon/Ticonderoga

Lake George

Fort William-Henry

NOVA SCOTIA

Halifax

BRITISH COLONIES   Boston

Fort Venango

Fort Duquesne

New York

Harbour

— British Positions
— French Positions

Louisbourg

British forces have surrounded the fortress
and have begun the bombardment of Louisbourg.

British Major-General Jeffrey Amherst. (Anne S. K. Brown Military Collection, Brown University Library)

Regiment went in against the French trenches garrisoned by the Royal Roussillon Regiment. After an hour of hard hand-to-hand fighting the attack was called off, and the British retreated back to the southern side of Lake George. The French had lost 350 men, while the British suffered 1,600 regulars and 334 provincial soldiers killed. In September, General Abercromby was replaced as Commander-in-Chief by Major-General Jeffrey Amherst.

The British did achieve some success on the New York frontier. A small unit of 2,000 men, under the command of Captain Bradstreet, launched an attack on the French Fort Frontenac on Lake Ontario on 25 August. The fort, which was a major supply depot for all the French forts in the western area of the Great Lakes and Ohio regions, fell only two days later. The bounty captured was approximately £800,000 sterling, and French communication between Quebec and the western forts was disrupted.

As it had been the previous year, Halifax was the main staging area for the attack on

Louisbourg. The British expedition, under the command of Major-General Jeffrey Amherst, comprised a force of 14 regular battalions of infantry as well as two specialist units of grenadiers and light infantry, numbering around 10,000 men. The Royal Navy had gathered 23 ships of the line and 10 frigates as well as numerous transport ships. The French had four battalions of regulars, 24 companies of Marines, and various Canadian militia units; 4,500 men in total, commanded by Governor Chevalier Augustin de Drucour. The French navy had five ships of the line and seven frigates.

The fortress at Louisbourg was very well defended. It had four defensive lines outside the walls, covering all the surrounding beaches. There were four bastions, Dauphin's, King's, Queen's, and Princess's, with 219 pieces of artillery and 17 mortars. The British landed on Freshwater Cove to the southwest of the fortress in the early morning of 8 June. The invasion force was divided into three brigades. The center brigade, under the command of Brigadier James Wolfe, landed first and encountered heavy opposition. An eyewitness account of the landing vividly noted the destructive capability of the French artillery fire:

One 24 pounder shot did a great deal of mischief. It passed under my hands and killed Sergeant McKenzie who was sitting as close to my left as he could squeeze … along with the shot [that] passed through Lt Cuthbert, who was on McKenzie's left … and cut off the legs of one of the fellows that held the tiller of the boat. (Harper, 78th Fighting Fraser's in Canada, pp. 42–43)

The center brigade was able to hold part of the beach and a second brigade was landed under the command of Brigadier Lawrence. This brigade was able to take the western trenches. The French, fearing that they were in danger of being cut off from the fortress, retreated with the British in hot pursuit until the latter were stopped by French artillery fire. General Amherst decided to lay siege, and he had succeeded in surrounding the fortress by 20 June when his troops captured the last French positions outside the fortress to the north. The Royal Navy, in addition to giving fire support to the troops on land, destroyed the French island battery in the harbor on 25 June. Six French ships were intentionally sunk by the French to blockade the entrance to the harbor, and with this move the French were completely surrounded.

On 9 July the defenders made a sortie against the British trenches. Seven hundred French attacked and carried the first line, but the British counter-attack forced the French to retreat to the fortress. By mid-July the British had begun to clear the remaining French trenches close to the walls. The British artillery, by utilizing the trenches and bastions closer to the walls of the fortress, was able to lay an effective bombardment, and the French commander began to make overtures towards surrender, eventually capitulating on 1 August. The British had lost 500 men killed and 1,000 men wounded. The French are estimated to have lost 1,000 killed and 2,000 wounded. More significantly, the British capture of Louisbourg meant that the way was opened to attack the heart of New France via the St Lawrence River.

The last major campaign in North America, although smaller in scale than the previous two, was significant in two ways. First, the army that attacked the area around Fort Duquesne was a different force from its 1755 counterpart. The British army had learned from its defeat and applied the tactics of forest fighting to its regular units. Second, Fort Duquesne was the original issue that had sparked the war, and putting it into British hands would change the political picture considerably.

A force of two British regular battalions and a number of provincial units, numbering 4,000 men, was tasked with building a road to Fort Duquesne and seizing the fort. As noted in the papers of the commander of the 4th Battalion, the 60th Foot, Royal American Regiment, the style of march was different from that of Braddock's campaign. The men were ordered as follows:

At the front of the column were a corporal and six woodsmen [cutting down trees], a guide a half a mile ahead, one sergeant and another twelve woodsmen a quarter of a mile back, and the rest of the column an additional quarter mile back. The first men were a Lt and a sergeant, with thirty men marching in Indian file. A corps of hatchet men would follow behind them with a company of soldiers for protection, followed up immediately by an artillery unit ... on all sides of the advance, including the front and back, were two man detachments, acting as skirmishers, who were not to go out of sight of the main column. (Bouquet Papers, II, pp. 657–8)

Throughout the summer the force advanced, building the new road and small forts along the way to protect the road and serve as supply depots for the army. By early September the force was close to Fort Duquesne.

Both sides sent small patrols out to skirmish with each other. On 14 September the British suffered a setback when the French garrison attacked their position, causing their provincial units to disperse and forcing them back to Fort Ligionier. The French sent a force of 400 troops to pursue and attack the retreating British, but the British had regrouped and were able to repel them easily. The British made another push towards Fort Duquesne at the end of October and by 24 November they were only a few miles away. From this vantage point they were able to witness the French, who had been ordered to withdraw to Venango, blowing up the fort. The British rebuilt the fort and renamed it Fort Pitt (the site of present-day Pittsburgh).

Western Europe

The British government refused to ratify the Convention of Kloster Zeven, which had stipulated the dissolution of the Hanoverian Allied army and permitted the French army to occupy most of Hanover. They knew that allowing Hanover to be occupied by the French would mean losing any colonial gains in exchange for its return in any future peace

settlement. The Allied army was to be
re-raised, under the command of Prince
Ferdinand of Brunswick, the brother-in-law of
Frederick II. Ferdinand held a Prussian
commission and had seen service in the earlier
campaigns of the war as well as at Rossbach.

While talks were taking place regarding
the resumption of war in the Hanover
region, the outcome of the Battle of
Rossbach demonstrated that a new campaign
was feasible. By late November 1757, the
Allied army was re-forming. The British
government had again agreed to pay for its
upkeep, but at present no British army units
were attached. Ferdinand spent November
and December training the army and raising
its morale. A French army corps, under the
command of Louis François Armand du
Plessis, Duc de Richelieu, who had replaced
d'Estrées as commander, marched against the
newly formed army. However, Ferdinand had
moved first. Seizing the initiative, he threw
back the various French garrisons who had
been in winter quarters, suffering from lack
of supplies and reinforcements.

Prince Ferdinand of Brunswick. (Anne S. K. Brown
Military Collection, Brown University Library)

Ferdinand was able to outmaneuver the French and seize territory that would be used as a firm base for future operations. On 18 February 1758 he recaptured the town of Hanover and by the end of March the electorate had been cleared of French troops. The campaign lasted only six weeks and the French retreated back across the Rhine. The campaign had cost the French dear. Their losses in numbers killed, wounded, and deserted were 16,000 men, while Ferdinand had lost only 200. Morale had been restored to the Allied army, while French morale had been devastated.

The rest of the year was spent with marches and countermarches between the two armies, as each side attempted to gain a significant advantage. Ferdinand's army, now renamed His Britannic Majesty's Army in Germany, had reached 40,000 men by the end of May. On 3 August, the first British army contingent arrived to join the new army. It consisted of six cavalry regiments and five battalions of infantry,

and signified Britain's commitment to the continental campaign. By this point, the campaign had already redrawn the strategic map in the western theater of operations. Hanover had been cleared of the French and Frederick's right flank was secure. The rest of the campaign would be characterized by a series of maneuvers by both sides. Ferdinand's army sought to deny the French access to Hanover and the western flank of Prussia. The French army sought to catch Ferdinand's army in a large pincer, destroy it, and thus occupy Hanover. The war in Hanover was instrumental in tying down large numbers of French soldiers who were needed in the war in the colonies.

Battle of Zorndorf, 25 August 1758. C and E) Prussian left wing attacks the Russian right flank. The attack goes badly as the Prussian units become separated. Russians launch a counterattack. The Prussian cavalry under the command of Lieutenant-General Seydlitz counterattack and restore the situation. F) The Prussian right flank attacks the Russian positions. (Christchurch Library)

Vorstellung der Bataille zwischen den Preußl u Rußen den 25 Aug.

Veſtung Cuſtrin

Zorndorf

Central Europe

While the Prussians held the initiative at the beginning of 1758, the year proved to be a dangerous and bloody one for them. Ferdinand's success meant that Prussia did not have to deal with a French enemy, but she had still to face a Russian attack at the heartland of the Prussian state which inflicted more damage upon the Prussians than anyone had thought possible. Prussia found herself fighting only two major battles, Zorndorf and Hochkirch, in 1758, but the price in terms of the loss of men and of the ability to deliver a decisive blow against the enemy was very high indeed.

Frederick decided to strike against the Austrians first, since he thought that the Russians would not move against him until the summer. He took the last Austrian stronghold in Silesia, Schweidnitz, in mid-April, and then invaded Moravia with 130,000 troops. His object was to lay siege to the important town of Olmütz. The siege dragged on, however, and in late June a large Prussian convoy en route to reinforce the siege was attacked and destroyed by an Austrian corps. Frederick knew that the siege was taking longer than he had wished, and he had also received reports that the Russians were on the move toward the Oder River. He decided to pull away from Olmütz and engage the Russians instead.

General Apraksin had been relieved of his command of the Russian troops and replaced by General Villim Villimovich Fermor. Fermor had been in command of the Russian army that reoccupied East Prussia over the winter of 1757–58. The Russian army marched from

Battle of Zorndorf, 25 August 1758. (Anne S. K. Brown Military Collection, Brown University Library)

On 25 August the Prussian and Russian armies met near the village of Zorndorf. Fermor had placed his 43,000 men in a marshy hollow that was surrounded on all sides by hills. The Prussian army arrived to the north of the Russian positions, then moved around to the south in an attempt to catch them from behind. However, Fermor was able to switch his lines around and face the Prussians. Frederick decided to attempt a flanking attack, with the left wing of his army applying the pressure. The Prussians opened with heavy artillery fire. A published account stated:

...[A]t nine o'clock in the morning the battle began by a fire of cannon and mortars which rained down on the right wing of the Russians without the least intermission for two hours. Nothing could exceed the havoc made by this terrible fire, nor the consistency with which the Muscovite foot ... sustained a slaughter that would have confounded and dispersed the compleatest veterans. (Annual Register, 1762)

At 11.00 am eight Prussian battalions launched a counterattack against the Russian right wing, hoping to turn it. The Russians launched an attack against the Prussians, which forced the Prussian left to shift itself towards the center of the Russians, contrary to the original orders. The Russians put in a flanking attack against the Prussian left. The Prussian Lieutenant-General Seydlitz attacked with a force of cavalry to restore the situation. The Russians pulled back from this, but continued to fight. The Prussian right wing began to move forward, but this attack did not gain much ground either. The battle descended into the confusion of hand-to-hand combat.

Sir Andrew Mitchell stated 'that no quarter was to be given, which rendered them [the Russians] desperate, and they fought like devils' (Mitchell's Journal regarding Zorndorf). Seydlitz was used in the center to push back any Russian cavalry charges that materialized against the Prussian center. The battle deteriorated into

East Prussia into Poland in large columns, and reports reached the Prussians that it was destroying everything in its path. The British envoy, Sir Andrew Mitchell, wrote that 'the [Prussian] soldiers are greatly animated against the Russians for the barbarities they have committed everywhere; and if action should ensue ... it will be a bloody one' (Mitchell to Holdernesse, 18/8/58). There was one Prussian corps of 26,000 men – under the command of Lieutenant-General Christoph v. Dohna, who had relieved Lehwaldt of command – near the Oder River. Frederick marched with 11,000 men to take over command of the Oder detachment, leaving the rest of his army in Silesia to counter any Austrian attacks. The two Prussian armies met on 22 August and proceeded to the east side of the Oder in search of the approaching Russian army.

Prussian prisoners guarded by Russians, c. 1758. (Anne S. K. Brown Military Collection, Brown University Library)

small pockets of men attempting to gain ground until evening, when both armies finally drew back, leaving the 'field of battle occupied by the dead' (Mitchell's Journal regarding Zorndorf). The Russians withdrew first and Mitchell rode with Frederick over the battlefield in the wake of their departure. He wrote afterwards, 'I will make no description as I heartily wish to forget it' (Mitchell's Journal regarding Zorndorf). The battle was a draw: the Prussians had lost 13,000 men and the Russians 19,000.

Artillery fire continued during the night and into the next morning. Neither side had the energy or willpower to attack on 26 August, but the armies remained close to one another until 1 September.

Following this engagement, Frederick turned his attention to the Austrians, marching into Saxony with elements of his army from Zorndorf. He met up with a Prussian force of 24,000 men. The Austrians had assembled a corps of 80,000 men under the command of Marshal Leopold J. v. Daun and they marched into Saxony as well, where the two armies spent five weeks attempting to outmaneuver one another.

taking its toll, and the Prussians, realizing they were running out of ammunition, began to withdraw. In spite of their initial success, the Austrians had been badly shaken by the heavy fighting and failed to pursue the retreating Prussians. The Prussians lost 9,000 men and the Austrians 8,000 men.

The Austrian army next moved against Dresden and laid siege. This did not last long because Daun, upon receiving news that a reinforced Prussian army was moving against him, withdrew to the fortified town of Pirna. The year 1758 ended on a good note for Frederick. He had cleared the Russians from the heart of Prussia and forced the Austrians to withdraw from Silesia and most of Saxony. In the process, however, his army was being bled white. The previous three years of war had accounted for the loss of close to 100,000 men, most of them highly trained veterans.

Indian subcontinent

In 1758 fighting in the Indian subcontinent shifted to the Carnatic region. The town of Pondicherry was the French administrative center, while Madras filled the same role for the British. Late in 1757, the French had been reinforced by 1,000 regular French troops, and this had forced the British in Madras to switch to the defensive, Britain being unable to send reinforcements to the region at this time. In April 1758, a French fleet and reinforcements under command of General Count Lally de Tollendal arrived at the French port of Pondicherry, where he was issued with the following specific orders: 'war will be waged against fortifications and maritime settlements of the English. English soldiers captured will be sent home to England and not allowed to stay in India' (Orme Collection, Vol. 27). A brief naval engagement occurred on 2 April between nine French and seven British ships. The outcome was indecisive, although the French lost more men. On the same day, a French force of 1,000 Europeans and 1,000 Sepoys attacked the British fort of Cuddalore, near Fort St David. Over the course of the next few days, the French were reinforced, and the

The armies met on the morning of 14 October near the village of Hochkirch. A Prussian soldier stated that skirmishing occurred at 3.30 am and that the order was given 'Fall in! Under Arms!' (Paret, *Frederick the Great: A Profile,* p. 122). Because Frederick initially thought he was facing only Austrian light troops and not the main army, some of the Prussian units had not formed into position when the Austrian attack came in against their camp at 5.00 am. The Austrian left pushed the Prussians back beyond the village of Hochkirch, while the Prussian left flank came under attack by a large Austrian force, taking the village of Koditz. The Austrian push against the Prussian flanks was

siege began in earnest. The garrison consisted of only 500 East India Company Sepoys, and capitulated on 4 May. The French moved on to Fort St David, which surrendered on 2 June. In the wake of these defeats, the British pulled all of their troops from the surrounding garrisons and gathered them in Madras.

Call to arms. (Anne S. K. Brown Military Collection, Brown University Library)

Lally spent the summer months attacking the countryside around Madras. As he needed money for his troops and naval forces, his men also illegally seized Dutch shipping and commerce to increase revenue. On 3 August the British Admiral Edward Pocock engaged the French navy under the command of Commodore Count Anne Antoine d'Ache and inflicted a defeat on the French at the Battle of Negapatam. The fleet

retreated to Pondicherry and remained in port for most of the campaign.

The British were reinforced in the autumn by Draper's 79th Foot, which enabled them to hold on to the strategic post at Conjeveram. Lally, with a force comprising 2,300 Europeans and 5,000 Sepoys, decided to move against the British at Madras and Fort St George. The British defenders numbered 1,750 Europeans and 2,200 Sepoys, under the command of Colonel Stringer Lawrence. By 13 December the French had arrived on the outskirts of the town, and heavy fighting broke out in the city streets on the 14th. Following this engagement, both sides withdrew from the city; the British pulled back into the fort, and the French began to build fortifications and lay siege to the fort. The siege, which continued for two months, was unsuccessful for the French. A British naval squadron arrived with reinforcements off Madras on 16 February 1759, and on 17 February, Lally withdrew towards Pondicherry as the British naval force sailed south.

1759

North America
The British planned small-scale attacks against the western forts of New France at the same time as the larger operations they launched against Fort Carillon and Quebec City. At the end of May, companies of three regular battalions marched towards Fort Niagara. The main British force, under the command of Brigadier Prideaux, arrived at Fort Niagara on 7 July and immediately laid siege. The French garrison numbered 110 men from the regular battalions, 180 men from the Marines, and 100 Canadian militia, under the command of Captain M. Pouchot. There was heavy skirmishing on both sides as the British trenches were dug. By 16 July the British had begun to bombard the fort. The British commander Prideaux was accidentally killed by a British mortar round and Sir William Johnson assumed command. The French commander noted that 'their musketry

considerably annoyed our batteries' (Pouchot, *Memoir of the Late War in North America between the French and the English*, p. 189). The British defeated a French relieving force of 800 men on 24 July, and the fort surrendered two days later.

The other French forts on the Ohio were also evacuated during July, with the escaping French troops withdrawing west towards Fort Detroit. The British had ejected the French from the Ohio valley, and with the earlier capture of Fort Frontenac, Lake Ontario became a staging post for a western drive to Montreal.

General Amherst and 11,000 British soldiers assembled at the south end of Lake George on 21 July and sailed north to lay siege to Fort Carillon. The French commander, Colonel Bourlamanque, and his garrison of 3,500 men destroyed the works, withdrew from the fort on 26 July, and fell back farther north. Amherst repaired the damage and renamed the fort Ticonderoga. All of Lake George was now in British hands.

British forces next moved against the French Fort St Frederic at Crown Point, farther up the west bank of Lake Champlain, but on 1 August news arrived that the French had abandoned this post as well and had withdrawn to Isle aux Noix, at the northern end of the lake. The British still needed to build a flotilla of ships for their proposed attack on the northern end of Lake Champlain and the campaign season was drawing to a close. It appeared that the advance towards Montreal via the lake would have to wait until the 1760 campaign season.

After passing through the dangerous waters of the lower St Lawrence river, the British arrived near Quebec on 21 June with 21 ships of the line, 22 frigates and sloops, close to 100 transports, 11 regular battalions of infantry, various provincial units and engineers, all commanded by Major General James Wolfe. The safe arrival of Wolfe's force was due in no small measure to the accuracy of the survey of the St Lawrence carried out by James Cook, master of the *Pembroke* and later to win renown as an explorer of the Pacific. The French commander, Montcalm, had called in reserves from the countryside, and the total number of defenders was

Battle of Quebec, 13 September 1759. The fortifications to the northeast of the city (upper right) are clearly shown. (National Army Museum, Chelsea)

around 15,000 men – 4,000 regulars, 1,000 Marines and the rest militia. Eight frigates of the French navy were also present.

The British landed unopposed on Ile d'Orléans on 26 June, and deployed troops opposite the French trenches along the Montmorency river on 10 July. The French had deployed troops in the city itself and also to positions in the northeast, heavily fortified with trenches and redoubts. On 31 July, a British attack was sent against the French trenches near the Montmorency Falls. This short engagement ended in defeat for the British, who lost over 500 men killed. Wolfe wished to draw the French defenders out to battle; however, Montcalm decided not to be drawn.

As autumn approached, Wolfe had to decide whether to attack the city or

withdraw until the following year. He decided to land his troops behind the city on the north side of the river. Quebec City and the fortress were located on a high hilltop. The city had a cliff face to the south, which dropped down to the river shore. Wolfe placed some of his troops in landing craft and sailed them up and down the river in early September, trying to reconnoiter for a possible landing place. On the evening of 12–13 September, a likely spot was selected.

Their movements undetected by the French, the ships landed the men unopposed on the chosen site. By 5.00 am on 13 September, the first British light infantry had scaled the cliffs and reached the top. At 7.00 am large numbers of British soldiers were entering the Plains of Abraham behind the city of Quebec. Montcalm ordered five of his regular battalions and various militia units toward the plain and by 9.00 am the French forces had assembled in linear formation. The British were also deployed in

linear formation, with some troops acting as skirmishers to the north of their position.

At 10.00 am Montcalm gave the order to advance. Wolfe had ordered that the British were not to open fire until the French were within 40yds (37m). The French fired at 130yds (119m), still too far away to cause any serious damage to the British line. The French kept advancing, firing sporadically, while the British waited. Finally, when they were close enough, two British battalions opened fire, causing serious damage in the French lines. The British line then advanced and opened fire, and the second volley caused further damage. Some eyewitness accounts said it sounded as if one large cannonball had been shot. The French line began to disperse and fall back toward the fortress, pursued by the British. Major General Wolfe was killed as the British pushed toward the retreating French lines. Montcalm was wounded at around the same time and died the next morning.

The city of Quebec capitulated to the British on 18 September. The British had lost 61 killed and 600 wounded, while the French are estimated to have lost close to

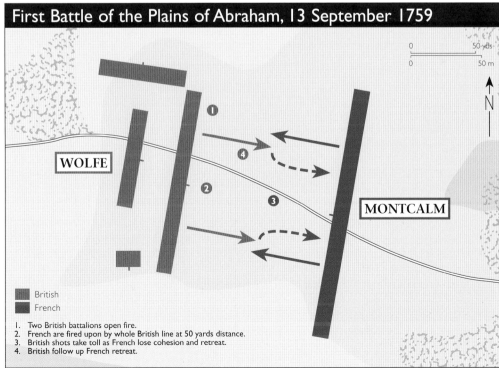

First Battle of the Plains of Abraham, 13 September 1759

WOLFE

MONTCALM

■ British
■ French

1. Two British battalions open fire.
2. French are fired upon by whole British line at 50 yards distance.
3. British shots take toll as French lose cohesion and retreat.
4. British follow up French retreat.

French Marshal Victor-François, Duc de Broglie. (Anne S.
K. Brown Military Collection, Brown University Library)

1,000 killed, wounded, and taken prisoner.
Even so, the French army in New France was
not yet completely defeated. Some units
besieged the British in Quebec during the
winter months, while the majority withdrew
to Trois-Rivières and Montreal for winter
quarters.

Western Europe

Ferdinand opened the campaign season of
1759 by attacking the French near Frankfurt
and Wesel, and the two armies met at Bergen
on 13 April. Ferdinand exhibited rash
behavior during the battle; he rushed his
forces into attack without proper time to
assemble or receive artillery support. In spite
of this, neither side managed to strike a
decisive blow. The French stayed on the

battlefield, expecting another attack, so Ferdinand was able to retreat with most of his army intact.

The French decided to move again toward Hanover in early June. The French army, numbering 60,000 men under the command of Marshal Louis Georges Erasme Contades, moved first. A second French force under the command of Marshal Victor-François, Duc de Broglie, which numbered 20,000 men, was held in reserve. From mid-June both forces were on the move against Ferdinand's army, which numbered around 35,000 men. Ferdinand moved north, trying to keep

Austrian Lieutenant-General Gideon Ernst v. Loudon. (Anne S. K. Brown Military Collection, Brown University Library)

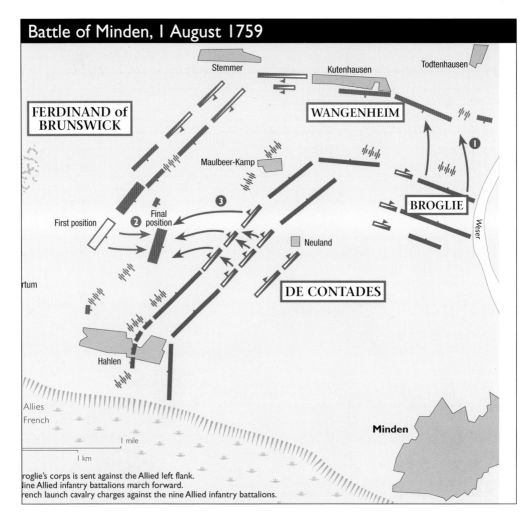

Battle of Minden, 1 August 1759

Stemmer

Kutenhausen

Todtenhausen

FERDINAND of BRUNSWICK

WANGENHEIM

Maulbeer-Kamp

BROGLIE

Weser

First position

Final position ②

③

Neuland

rtum

DE CONTADES

Hahlen

Allies
French

1 mile

1 km

Minden

roglie's corps is sent against the Allied left flank.
line Allied infantry battalions march forward.
rench launch cavalry charges against the nine Allied infantry battalions.

Contades' force within reach. Both sides attempted to outflank each other and cut off supply lines. Ferdinand intended to fall back towards Minden, which was a major supply depot, but Broglie's forces seized the town first in early July. This meant that Hanover was at risk, with Ferdinand and his army to the west of the French at Minden. The French stayed in the area, seizing supplies, and Ferdinand had to split his force to deal with the various French light troops scattered throughout the countryside.

By the end of July, Ferdinand was gathering his army together, although Marshal Contades was under the impression that they were dispersed throughout the countryside. When intelligence arrived that the Allies were making a move towards

Minden, Contades assembled his army for battle. On 31 July his orders stressed the importance of Broglie's right wing: 'the attack of this reserve will be quick and rapid in order to overcome Wangenheim's corps at once' (Mss King's 235). He intended by this attack to expose the left flank of Ferdinand's army. Contades also deployed his army in unusual formation, placing his infantry on the wings and his cavalry in the center. His troops had been ordered to stand to at 3.00 am. Broglie's corps began to march at 4.00 am on 1 August, but Ferdinand's troops were prepared for a possible attack and halted Broglie's advance. The two main armies continued moving into battlefield positions, and both sides began artillery bombardments.

Battle of Minden, 1 August 1759. The foreground clearly depicts the French cavalry charging the Allied infantry battalions. (Anne S.K. Brown Military Collection, Brown University Library)

As the two armies moved closer, the fire increased on both sides. Nine battalions of Ferdinand's infantry (three Hanoverian and six British battalions) moved ahead of the Allied lines, opposite the main French center made up of cavalry. The French artillery pounded the nine infantry battalions as they moved forward, while the Allied artillery on the infantry right flank gave covering fire. The destructive power of the artillery was noted by a British officer: 'we were not suffered to fire but stood tamely looking on whilst they at their leisure picked us off as you would small birds' (National Army Museum 6807-142-13).

The French launched 11 squadrons of cavalry against the nine Allied infantry battalions. The infantry held their fire until the French were within 30 feet (9m) and then opened up. The barrage caused the French to retreat in disorder. Contades tried to regroup, moving up infantry in an attempt to dislodge

the nine Allied infantry battalions. At the same time, a second French cavalry charge was ordered, only to be defeated by the Allied infantry. At this point Ferdinand ordered Lord Sackville, commander of the Allied cavalry, to charge. He failed to carry out the order and was duly replaced after the battle. The French infantry also failed. A British officer stated that the Allies 'discovered a large body of infantry consisting of 17 regiments moving down on our flank … our regiment wheeled and showed them a front which is a thing not to be expected from troops already twice attacked' (National Army Museum 7510-92). Ferdinand moved more infantry units forward to support the nine battalions. A third French cavalry attack came in and it too was broken.

By 11.00 am the struggle was over as the Allied left flank pushed back Broglie's wing. An officer of a British regiment wrote to his mother a few days after the battle. He stated: 'I don't care who knows my sentiments when I say my curiosity is satisfied and that I never wish to see a second slaughter of my fellow creatures' (National Army Museum

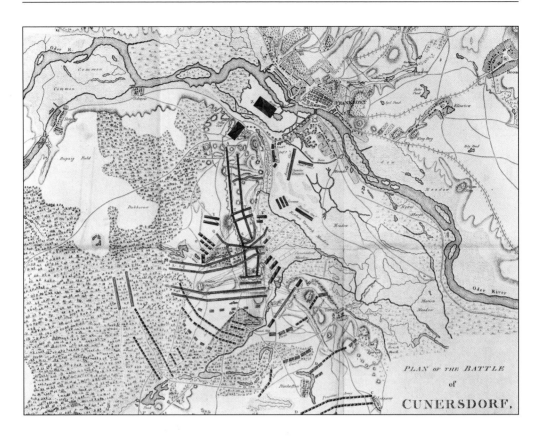

Battle of Kunersdorf, 12 August 1759. 1st image: L and B)
Prussians attack the Russian right flank. After heavy fighting
they carry the Russian positions at Muhl-Berge. 2nd Image:
N) Prussians follow up by attacking the Russian positions at
Kuh-Grund. The Russians have reinforced the position with
troops from farther down the line. The Prussians are not
able to break through and begin to fall back. O and X)
A Prussian cavalry charge is sent in to relieve pressure,
but it is attacked by joint Austrian/Russian cavalry and is
dispersed. The Russian artillery on Grosser-Spitzberg takes
a further toll on the Prussian cavalry. (Christchurch Library)

6807-142-13). The Allied army suffered
2,600 killed and wounded, many of whom
were members of the nine Allied battalions.
The French lost around 8,000 men.

After a series of marches and countermarches, the two armies entered winter
quarters with the same ground under their
command as they had held at the beginning
of the campaign season. Due to the Prussian
loss at Kunersdorf, Ferdinand was asked to
send reinforcements to Frederick, a
redeployment that limited Ferdinand's
offensive capabilities.

Central Europe

The Russians spent the early months of 1759
preparing their army for a new offensive into
Prussia. The Russian force, under the
command of General Petr Semenovich
Saltykov and numbering 50,000 men, set out
in late June. The Austrians sent a corps of
20,000 troops, under the command of
Lieutenant-General Gideon Ernst v. Loudon,
to join the Russian advance in a joint effort
to destroy the main Prussian field army in
one decisive campaign. On 23 July, the
Russian army met a Prussian corps and
soundly defeated them at Paltzig. Frederick,
upon hearing this news, marched with
19,000 men toward the remnants of the
defeated Prussian force. He arrived in early
August and took command of the Prussian
corps from the defeated Lieutenant-General
Johann Heinrich v. Wedell. His army now
numbered 50,000 men.

Both sides maneuvered for position near
the Oder river. Saltykov feared his army
being caught on the march by Frederick and

eventually decided to dig them in on a ridge near the village of Kunersdorf on the eastern side of the Oder River. A Prussian officer stated: 'they [the Russians] had occupied a very strong camp fortified and covered with cannon' (Lloyd, *History of the Late War in Germany*, II, 143).

The Prussians began to march on the Russian positions at 2.00 am on 12 August. They had not reconnoitered very well and were hoping to maneuver around the Russian lines and take them from the rear and left flank. However, the Russians had defended themselves on most sides with trenches and redoubts, and in the expectation that the attack would fall on this part of the ridge, Muhl-Berge, they had fortified the position with considerable artillery. The Prussians emerged and attacked the Russian left flank, from three sides. Although pounded by Russian artillery, the Prussians were able to seize the northeast area of the fortification.

Drawing of a Prussian officer (right) and a grenadier. In the background, Prussian drilling can be seen. (Anne S. K. Brown Military Collection, Brown University Library)

A second Prussian attack went in against Kuh-Grund, but this one was not successful, retreating under an onslaught of Russian artillery and musket fire. Frederick noted that 'the attack was several times received, but it was impossible to carry this battery, which commanded the whole ground' (Frederick II, *History of the Seven Years War*, II, p. 14). At midday a Prussian cavalry charge was sent in against the Grosser-Spitzberg line, but it too failed. Russian artillery fire raked its columns and a Russian/Austrian cavalry charge decimated the survivors. Soltykov stated: '[the] Prussians kept attacking and suffered heavily ... their lines had been exposed to artillery' (Lloyd, *History of the Late War in Germany*, II, pp. 147–8). By 6.00 pm the

British Colonel Eyre Coote. (Anne S. K. Brown Military Collection, Brown University Library)

Prussians had begun to withdraw from the battlefield, but the Russians failed to follow up the retreat and to destroy the Prussians completely.

Frederick had suffered 19,000 dead, wounded, and missing, while the joint Russian/Austrian army had suffered close to 15,000 dead and wounded. The Russian army crossed the Oder River intending to head east toward Berlin, but it was forced to detour south to assist another Austrian corps, who had had their line of communications cut by a small Prussian force. Relations between the Russian and Austrian armies were beginning to deteriorate, as is evidenced by a letter from the Russian commander to the Austrian commander, Daun:

I have done enough, sir for one year. I have gained two victories, which have cost the Russians 27,000 men. I only wait till you shall in like manner have gained two battles and I will begin anew. It is not just that troops of my sovereign should act singly. (Frederick II, History of the Seven Years War, *II, p. 33)*

Kunersdorf was Frederick's worst defeat, but not his last of 1759. He lost the strategic city of Dresden on 4 September and a Prussian corps of 13,000 at Maxen on 20 November. He and his army, tired and bled white as it was, were still in the field as 1759 drew to a close. The inability of the Austrian and Russian armies to stage a combined effort against Berlin and the remnants of the Prussian army were to prove decisive, enabling Frederick and his men to survive and prepare for another campaign season.

Indian subcontinent

There was minimal fighting on the subcontinent in 1759 as both sides rearmed and tried to strengthen their respective forces. Lally and his forces had to retreat toward Pondicherry as Madras was reinforced, and the French forces had threatened mutiny after going without pay for many months. The mutiny was put down peacefully, but 60 men escaped and joined the British forces. Two hundred British reinforcements arrived in June, and in the autumn Colonel Eyre Coote arrived with a further 1,000 troops. At this time he also took command of all His Majesty's and Company troops.

1760

North America

The British were poised to march on Montreal in the campaign of 1760. However, the British garrison in Quebec City had had a difficult winter and of its 5,600 troops, 2,300 had been ill. A large French force of 8,500 men, commanded by Major-General François-Gaston, Chevalier de Levis, arrived from Montreal in the early spring and laid siege to the city. The French hoped to defeat the British and retake the city before the ice broke on the St Lawrence River, allowing the Royal Navy to appear with reinforcements. The British commander, Major-General George Murray, decided to confront the French army assembling on the Plains of

Abraham on 28 April. The British garrison was soundly defeated, and retreated to the city to prepare its defense for the renewal of the French siege.

On 16 May, two Royal Navy ships arrived to relieve the British, forcing the French to lift the siege and retreat toward Montreal. The relief of the Quebec garrison by the Royal Navy was ultimately to play a larger role in determining the fate of Canada than the first Battle of the Plains of Abraham the previous September.

By mid-summer the British had launched three pincer movements on Montreal. The first headed up-river from Quebec City, the second came up from Lake Champlain, and the third was launched down the St Lawrence River from the west. The third pincer was the most important, as it was designed to block any French troops attempting to retreat from Montreal toward the west. By 6 September the three armies had converged and surrounded the island of Montreal, and on 8 September the French garrison surrendered to General Amherst.

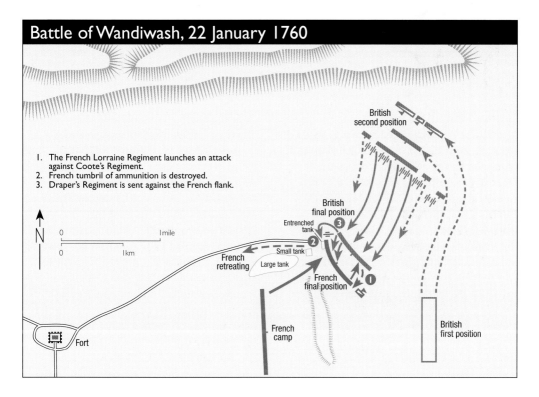

Battle of Wandiwash, 22 January 1760

1. The French Lorraine Regiment launches an attack against Coote's Regiment.
2. French tumbril of ammunition is destroyed.
3. Draper's Regiment is sent against the French flank.

Indian subcontinent

After Coote had assembled his newly formed army of two regular battalions and various Company European and Sepoy troops, he pushed out southward from Madras, successfully recapturing several former British positions. The French commander, Lally, had hoped that the newly arrived British forces would be sent north to Bengal to assist in defeating a move by the Dutch East India Company against the British. However, the British troops in Bengal were able to defeat the Dutch on 25 November 1759 without outside assistance, freeing Coote to center all his attention on defeating the French in the Carnatic. The two armies tried to outmaneuver one another and gain

tactical advantage until 22 January, when they met outside the fort of Wandiwash.

The Battle of Wandiwash was chiefly between the regular units of both armies, arrayed in continental linear style. A distinguishing feature of this engagement was that the native troops of the British were arrayed and equipped as European soldiers for the first time. Lally deployed his army with the European cavalry on the right wing; next to them was the Lorraine Regiment; the French East India Company European regiment was in the center; and Lally's own regiment was on the left flank. French native Sepoys were deployed behind the first line, and the total force numbered 4,000 men. Coote had deployed his force along similar

immediately on the flanks. The French launched the Lorraine Regiment against Coote's regiment; after a volley of musket fire, both sides engaged in heavy hand-to-hand fighting. The French retreated first after losing many men, and the battle was decided after a French tumbril of ammunition was destroyed by British artillery on the French left flank, causing the French line to lose cohesion.

Draper's regiment was then sent against the French flank to push home the advantage and turn the French line into the center, causing more destruction and loss of cohesion. An officer in Draper's regiment wrote: 'immediately we seized these guns which would otherwise have flanked and caused much mischief ... then drove a body of them ... and after a shower of musketry for two minutes sent them flying' (National Army Museum 7508-47). By 2.00 pm the French were in full retreat with their flanks taken. The French lost 600 men killed, wounded and taken prisoner; the British lost only 200 killed and wounded.

Coote's next objective was to concentrate on taking all the French outposts outside the key city of Pondicherry and then to besiege the city itself. After receiving reinforcements, Coote pressed against the last remaining French posts while the Royal Navy blockaded Pondicherry from the sea. On 15 January 1761, the French surrendered Pondicherry and their last major foothold in India.

Western Europe

The war between the French and Ferdinand's forces continued with outcomes much the same as in 1759. His Britannic Majesty's Army had been reinforced with a second British contingent in the spring and summer of 1760, numbering eight cavalry and 10 infantry regiments. There were many maneuvers as the French launched a major

lines, with the first line held by European Company troops in the center; Draper's Regiment were on their right and Coote's regiment on their left, with one battalion of Sepoys on both flanks. The second line was made up of a composite battalion of grenadiers, supported on both flanks by Sepoys, and the third line was made up of cavalry. The British numbered around 4,000 men. It is interesting to note that this decisive battle was fought with such small numbers of men, illustrating how both France and England were stretched to provide many regular troops to India due to requirements in other areas.

Both armies began to advance at 7.00 am, and skirmishing and artillery duels began

Austrian cavalry, both heavy (center) and light hussar troops (left and right). (Anne S. K. Brown Military Collection, Brown University Library)

attack intended to destroy Ferdinand's ability to wage another campaign. As the French closed in, Ferdinand was able to cause havoc in the lines of communication serving the large French corps.

After a series of maneuvers and counter-maneuvers, on 31 July near Warburg, Ferdinand's army caught up with a sizable French force, under the command of Lieutenant-General Le Chevalier du Muy. Ferdinand split his force into three with the object of outflanking the French positions. After a brief but sharp skirmish the French

began to withdraw. Ferdinand decided to employ his British cavalry under the command of Sir John Manners, the Marquis of Granby, against the French army center. The cavalry had to cover five miles (8km) in order to attack the French positions. Twenty-two squadrons of British cavalry smashed into the French cavalry and then their infantry lines, creating chaos. As a British soldier stated: 'they charged so well, that they soon made the French retreat, killed and drowned numbers and took a great many prisoners' ('John Tory's Journal,' *JOSAHR*, LIV, no. 218, p. 79). The Allied infantry was not able to keep up with the cavalry charge due to the terrain, which allowed the French to withdraw. The Allies

lost 1,200 men in the attack and the French lost 6,000 men killed, wounded or captured.

Both sides regrouped after Warburg, engaging in maneuvers and sending light troops out to disrupt each other's supply networks. The French in the early autumn moved north to attack Hanover from a different direction, and the two armies met at Kloster Kamp on 16 October. The fighting began early in the morning when the light troops of both armies encountered each other. The full armies of both sides were engaged in short order and throughout the morning sent in reinforcements to break the deadlock, only to have more soldiers bogged down. The battle favored one side then the other at different times, until a timely

French cavalry charge created serious disorder in the Allied infantry lines. This action forced a retreat and by midday the battle was over. Both sides had lost 3,000 men killed, wounded, and captured.

Ferdinand withdrew to Warburg after attempting further maneuvers to dislodge the French, and both armies settled into their winter quarters. The French had been unable to destroy the Allied army for another year, despite increased pressure on their commanders to defeat Ferdinand and win Hanover in the wake of territorial losses in New France and India.

Central Europe

The fighting began in Silesia when an Austrian corps under General Loudon defeated a Prussian corps at Landeshut on 23 June. The Austrians heavily outnumbered the Prussians, 34,000 men to 11,000. The Prussians were easily defeated, losing 10,000 men killed and captured. The Austrians then moved with two corps to destroy the main Prussian army. Field Marshal Daun and General Loudon marched and met, combining their forces near the village of Liegnitz. The Austrians numbered close to 90,000 men, while Frederick could muster only 30,000.

As the two Austrian corps converged upon the Prussians on 15 August, however, Frederick moved his positions at night to disrupt their plan of attack. Loudon met the Prussians first and was heavily beaten back, withdrawing after two hours. The main Austrian corps had failed to arrive to join battle, and without reinforcements Loudon's corps lost 8,000 men, while the Prussians lost 3,000. Frederick had once again demonstrated his ability to outmaneuver a larger force and not only survive, but also win victories.

Frederick was again in control of central Silesia. In the meantime, however, Russian and Austrian troops, in a rare joint operation, had launched an attack on Berlin with 35,000 troops. On 9 October their combined forces seized the city and demanded payment of tributes to the army.

Frederick moved toward Berlin with a corps and the raid ended three days later.

At this point, Daun moved the main Austrian army of 55,000 men into Saxony, and Frederick immediately set out to respond to this threat. He marched with 48,000 men, splitting his corps in two. One corps headed south to block any Austrian reinforcements coming north from Dresden, while Frederick marched the other corps to engage the Austrians from the rear near Torgau. The two armies met on 3 November. Daun had successfully anticipated Frederick's movements and moved his lines around accordingly.

Frederick launched the battle at 2.00 pm with an attack against the center of the Austrians. The Austrians beat back the attack with a heavy artillery cannonade. A second Prussian attack went in and it too was beaten. The Prussians, suffering heavy losses, appeared to be losing their spirit, when the second Prussian corps that had been detached earlier arrived at the scene of battle and came upon the Austrians from behind, turning the left flank. As night fell, the Austrians began to lose cohesion, eventually calling a general retreat and withdrawing towards Dresden. The Austrians and the Prussians had each lost 16,000 men.

The end of the war: 1761–63

The final years of the war were marked by both military and financial exhaustion, a growing will to end the conflict, struggles to gain territory, and the consequences of the death of the Empress Elizabeth of Russia. The war in the central theater of operations was characterized by Prussia's switch to a more defensive mode of operations – a desperate attempt to maintain her very existence as the Austrians and Russians amassed more armies to defeat her. With the death of Elizabeth and the subsequent withdrawal of Russia from the fray, Prussia was able to focus her dwindling resources against one enemy, Austria. The fighting in the western theater of operations had not changed

significantly. The French were desperate to seize Hanover as quickly as possible; they recognized that peace was close at hand and wished to have as large a bargaining advantage as possible at the peace talks. However, Ferdinand and the Allied army successfully staved off their attempts. The final theater of operations was the Spanish Empire. Spain, a last-minute ally of France, foolishly joined the belligerents, but her fleet and army were not prepared for entry into the conflict in 1762, and they were soon overwhelmed by the large and highly experienced combined operations team of the Royal Navy and British army.

Central Europe

Frederick's army in the last stages numbered more than 100,000 men, most of whom were raw recruits and prisoners of war incapable of the complex maneuvers and rapid marches that had allowed Frederick to strike at his enemies with vigor. To compensate for this, Frederick switched his strategy to positional warfare, in which he attempted to wear down his enemies with strategic use of fortifications and maneuvers.

Two large Russian and Austrian corps, totalling 130,000 men, moved against the Prussians in Silesia. Frederick began building a large fortified camp at Bunzelwitz, near Schweidnitz, on 20 August 1761. Inside the camp he stationed 66 battalions and 143 squadrons. The fort was heavily protected and the terrain denied the Austrians and Russians the use of their artillery. However, Frederick made one tactical error: thinking that the Austrians and Russians would not attack the camp, he withdrew most of his force and marched toward Neisee on 26 September. In his absence, on the night of 30 September, the Austrians seized Bunzelwitz.

Only the death of Empress Elizabeth of Russia on 5 January 1762 saved the Prussian state from destruction. Her son and successor, Grand Prince Peter, was an admirer of Frederick and sought peace with Prussia. The Treaty of St Petersburg of either 2 or 5 May freed Frederick to concentrate his energies

Prussian grenadiers led into battle. (Anne S. K. Brown Military Collection, Brown University Library)

The Caribbean

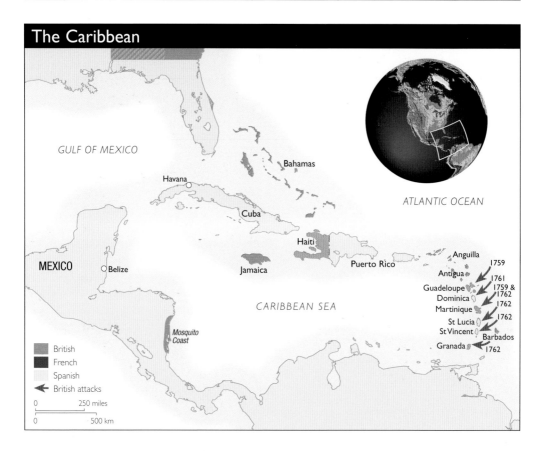

against the Austrians. Peter was dethroned by his wife, Catherine the Great, on 18 July. She wished to renew the war against Prussia, but in the end the Russians stayed neutral while the Prussians and Austrians fought for control of Silesia and Saxony, both sides knowing that peace could not be far off. The Prussians were able to gain the upper hand in both provinces, and with both sides exhausted, an Austrian messenger arrived to open negotiations on 29 November 1762.

Western Europe
The French poured more troops into the fight against Ferdinand and the Allied army, sensing that peace was close at hand. Ferdinand had launched a winter offensive in 1761, but over the course of the winter and early spring he had been pushed back to his original starting lines. As the spring approached, the French had amassed two large corps, totaling 130,000 men, commanded by Broglie and Soubise. On 16 July, the French army was

defeated at Vellinghausen, but Ferdinand was once again unable to turn the defeat into a rout. This failure allowed the French army to regain the initiative and attempt a strike against the major supply depots of the Allied army. After a series of marches and countermarches where both sides attempted to gain the advantage, the French offensive was finally stopped in early November. Ferdinand had succeeded in keeping the two French corps in constant motion for over six months with the Allied light troops disrupting the French lines of communication. Finally, Ferdinand and his exhausted troops launched a counteroffensive that cleared the French threat to Hanover within a week.

By the end of May 1762, both the French corps and the Allied army had been assembled for another campaign season. The major engagement of 1762 was at Wilhelmsthal on 24 June, where the Allied army surprised the French army in their camp and inflicted another defeat. While all did not go according to plan for the Allies on the battlefield, this victory forced the French offensives in the region to come to a standstill. Late in the campaign season, the Allied army marched north to besiege Cassel. On 1 November the town capitulated, and news arrived shortly thereafter that peace negotiations had begun between the French and British governments.

War with Spain and France

By the spring of 1761, the French court had approached the British government with offers of a peace. However, there were signs that there had been a secret agreement between the French and Spanish courts about a possible Spanish entry to the war. Upon receiving this information, the British government withdrew from negotiations and planned an attack on Spain. It seemed too good an opportunity to miss, to sweep the Spanish from the seas as well.

The British launched a combined force against the Spanish and French colonies in the Caribbean and the Philippines. A large part of the force consisted of British troops from North America who had participated in the victories in Canada and India. The combined operations of the Royal Navy and British army had been developed to a high level of professionalism over the previous few years. The French island of Guadeloupe had been seized in an earlier expedition in 1759, and was used as a forward base when the campaign against Dominica began in June 1761. Dominica surrendered on 7 June. Early in 1762 the fleet and army attacked the island of Martinique, which surrendered after heavy fighting on 12 February. After other smaller islands had been seized, the main British fleet and army were in sight of Havana on 6 June. After a year most of the Caribbean islands were in British hands.

A squadron of six British ships of the line blockaded the Spanish ships in Havana harbor. By July, British forces had surrounded Havana and begun a bombardment, which ended only when the Spanish guns had been silenced on 10 August. For the British, the greatest threat in this campaign was disease; they lost 1,000 killed and wounded to the

George III of Great Britain. (Ann Ronan Picture Library)

Spanish defenders, compared with more than 5,000 men lost to illness by October.

France had monitored British movements and, after British troops had been withdrawn for the operations in the West Indies, a French naval squadron and 1,500 troops seized Newfoundland on 27 June 1762. The colony had vital fishing grounds, and once more the French motivation was to gain territorial bargaining chips for peace negotiations. Their strategy was ultimately unsuccessful, as the British had regained Newfoundland by force by mid-September.

The attack on Manila in the Spanish Philippines originated from the British stationed in India. The force comprised 1,000 European troops (half Company and half King's troops) and 2,000 Sepoys. The invasion force arrived and laid siege to Manila on 25 September 1762, and a bitter

A good illustration of British combined operations at work at Havana, 7 June 1762. (National Maritime Museum)

fight ensued, enlivened by many Spanish counterattacks. On 6 October the British succeeded in creating a breach in the city wall and after this, as noted by an officer of the campaign, 'assault was so sudden that they had no time to oppose us on the breech and bastion but they retreated towards their houses' (Orme Collection, Vol. 32).

After losing Manila, the Spanish surrendered all their possessions in the Philippine Islands, concentrating their energy on Britain's ally, Portugal, which they had invaded in April 1762. The British responded quickly, swiftly moving in reinforcements of 7,000 men and attaching British officers to the Portuguese army. The British were able to stop the invasion and inflict heavy casualties, but they were unable to destroy the Spanish completely or to push them out of Portugal.

both nations had agreed not to negotiate with any party unless both approved, but Britain violated this understanding when she began to make overtures to the French. This readiness to break obligations later caused a serious rift in relations between Prussia and Britain.

The Seven Years' War was finally brought to an end with two separate peace treaties. The first, the Treaty of Paris, involved Great Britain, France, and Spain and was signed on 10 February 1763. Under its terms, Britain was granted Canada, Cape Breton Island, Newfoundland, the Ohio River valley, and all the land to the east of the Mississippi River. France renounced all claims to New France, receiving in exchange only two islands off the coast of Newfoundland, St Pierre and Miquelon. France also received Martinique, Guadeloupe, and Marie Galante in the Caribbean, while Britain retained Grenada and all the Lesser Antilles except for St Lucia. Britain also became the dominant European power in the Carnatic and Bengal regions of India, for while Pondicherry had been returned to the French, it could not be fortified. Belle Isle (off the coast of France) was given back to France in return for Minorca, and the British returned Goree, in West Africa, in exchange for Senegal. France also agreed to evacuate all of the German territories of George III and his allies. Britain returned Cuba and the Philippines to Spain in return for Florida and withdrawal from Portugal.

The Austrians and Prussians signed the Peace Treaty of Hubertusburg on 15 February 1763. All the borders of 1756 were reinstated; Austria evacuated Silesia, and Prussia withdrew her troops from Saxony. Frederick acknowledged that no territory had been gained, but the two main war aims of Austria and Russia had not been realized. Silesia remained part of Prussia, and the dismemberment of Prussia as a state had not happened. In fact, the opposite was true: the war had considerably strengthened Prussia's role as a major European power.

With the accession of George III to the British throne in 1760, British strategy began to change. George III cared more about the war in the colonies and less about the war in Germany. By October 1761, the British governmental alliance of William Pitt and the Duke of Newcastle that had promoted a joint colonial/continental war had come to an end. Lord Bute became the chief minister, and at this point the British began to abandon Prussia both politically and monetarily. Originally

British siege battery at Havana, 1762.
(National Maritime Museum)

A soldier of the British 68th Regiment of Foot

This section draws upon an unnamed soldier's journal which describes the British attacks on the coast of France in 1758. As with the operations of 1757, this engagement was an attempt to draw off French forces from the western European theater of operations. This soldier describes the events of that summer; he gives excellent insight into camp life, rations in the fleet and lack of training. He also highlights the difficulty of combined operations, when troops are caught without artillery support. Sadly, the author never mentioned his own name in the journal or its date of publication, so we can determine very little about the person who wrote this account.

The soldier was born in Oxford in 1743. In April 1758 he enlisted at the age of 15 into the 68th Regiment of Foot. He may have made a mistake about the regimental number, since although the 68th did serve in the coastal operations of 1758, it was not involved in the first embarkation of which he was part, but only the second and third operations. He describes how in May he set out with other recruits to travel to the Isle of Wight from Dover, seeking to attract other recruits on the way.

The soldier describes his arrival on the Isle of Wight, and mentions, interestingly for the era, that the regiments were placed in tented towns and not quartered with the population. A very detailed account is given of how the camps were set up, including the following relevant items. All of the men were given equipment to set up their tents, and were to gather straw for their own beds. Six men were assigned to each tent, and two blankets were given to each man. The usual arrangement for sleeping was head to foot, so that three faced one way and three the other. The accepted rule was that the oldest soldier slept farthest away from the entrance, and the youngest slept next to it, which obviously meant being trodden upon.

He then explains the regiment and how they camped. Each regiment in theory had eight companies plus two grenadier companies. Each company formed a street, and each side of the street consisted of 10 tents whose entrances faced one another. The sergeants' tents were at the front and faced the front of the camp, one to each 10. All the men's muskets were kept in front of the sergeants' tent at the bell-tent. The grenadiers formed two half-streets on the flanks of the other eight companies, and in the center of the front were the drums and colors of the regiment.

The quarter guard was at 150 paces in front of the rest of camp. It had an officers' marquee and six to eight tents for the guards. These tents were purposely placed on this spot to prevent desertion from the regiment. In the rear of the men's tents was the subalterns' line of marquees, then the captains', and lastly the field officers'. Behind this was the officers' mess.

When the soldier first arrived, he was examined by a doctor. The men then paraded in front of the officers, who allocated them to regiments by drawing numbers from a hat. He was drawn for the second battalion, the 68th Foot, and provided with a red coat, laced hat, cap, gun, sword, etc. The next day he was taken out to learn how to walk (the art of learning maneuvers), and then to learn how to use a musket. All this happened in one day, and he had been in camp for only 11 days when orders arrived to embark. If this few days' instruction was the norm for learning very complicated maneuvers, it is not surprising that newly arrived recruits were considered to be deficient in training.

The soldier's journal next gives a very detailed list of provisions on board ship. On Mondays, six men were given 4lbs (1.8kg) of bread, half a pound (0.23kg) of cheese, and three-quarters of a pound (0.34kg) of butter. On Tuesday they received 4lbs of beef, 4 lbs of flour, and 1lb (0.45kg) of fruit plus bread. On Wednesday the men were given the same menu as Monday. On Thursday the men were given 2lbs (0.9kg) of pork instead of beef. The Saturday menu was the same as Tuesday, and the Sunday menu was the same as Thursday. The men appear to have been better fed than is commonly believed today.

The fleet numbered 24 ships of the line and the army strength was numbered at 13,000 men. The fleet arrived on 5 June opposite Cancalle Bay near St Malo and the troops were landed the following day. The soldier wrote that he was 'given provisions for three days'. He also describes how 'for six hours the ships kept ferrying men ashore'. He comments that there were only about 100 French in the area, and describes how in the town of Cancalle, 'all the people fled so the sailors and soldiers plundered and some were caught and one was hung.' Most of the army then marched off toward St Malo, but his regiment, along with one other, remained at Cancalle. The troops advancing on St Malo destroyed shipping in the area.

The soldier mentions that 'from 3 a.m. to late in the evening the two regiments in Cancalle were busy building defensive works.' The troops sent to St Malo were re-embarked as news arrived of a larger French force, and the soldier states that his regiment re-embarked also from Cancalle. The fleet headed toward Cherbourg, 'weather intervened however and the ships sailed back to Portsmouth.'

The soldier briefly mentions the second embarkation, which arrived off Cherbourg on 6 August. A force was sent ashore and fought an engagement on 7 August, repelling the French and allowing the rest of the force to land on the next day. The town of Cherbourg surrendered and the port installations were destroyed. The troops were then re-embarked.

On 3 September the fleet arrived at St Lunaire Bay, near St Malo. The force was again unable to mount a proper siege of St Malo, and the soldier spends most of his time describing the coming disaster. He describes how, as the British formed a camp after an engagement with the French, they captured French deserters. The deserters warned that a large French force was soon to arrive. He passed this information along to his officers, but they did not express much concern. On 11 September orders were given to embark the troops, but boarding proceeded in a casual fashion. He describes what followed:

the French army appeared, and in the short time they began to cannonade us, which we could not return, having no artillery on shore, but the shipping did for us all that was possible to be done; by the time our regiment began to embark, the shot flew both thick and hot, and every boat made to the first ship they could reach, the boat that I was in got on board one of the bomb ketches, who the minute we came along side of her, discharged a 13 inch mortar, the shell of which I saw fall in the middle of a troop of French horse. By this time the action became general among the troops we had on shore and a dreadful scene it was! To see so many brave fellows lose their lives, and we not able to give them any manner of assistance, at last the few who remained were obliged to throw down their weapons and surrender.

The 68th Foot returned to England, and the soldier's regiment spent the winter at Rochester. In April 1759 the regiment served garrison duty on the island of Jersey, then it was shipped to Guadeloupe island, to fulfill the same role, in the spring of 1760. There it remained for more than three years, returning to England on 23 August 1763. The soldier was discharged on 28 September of the same year, at the age of 20.

The civilian and economic cost

While historians feel that it is still classifiable as a limited war of the eighteenth century, the Seven Years' War had elements of total war. Chiefly notable are the crippling economic burdens that many of the combatants assumed just to keep their armies in the field, but the effects upon the civilian populations are also significant.

The civilians in the various theaters of operations suffered greatly, especially if they were caught in a war zone. Although their fellow citizens suffered from taxes and food shortages, they did not have to contend with the military forces at first hand. All of the armies were guilty of abusing the local civilian populations. Supply breakdowns and lack of money to pay for forage drove many armies to pillaging the local communities. Most of this occurred in enemy territory, but it was not uncommon for armies to seize supplies from areas they had been engaged to protect.

The war in the western theater of operations displays numerous examples of pillaging and abuse by both sides. The British forces who first joined His Britannic Majesty's Army in Germany in 1758 were noted for their insolent behavior in Hanover, notably rude behavior to civilians because they were not British. The local German population, for their part, charged inflated rates for the army's forage, and there were reported cases of the British forces pillaging local areas. However, the French forces in the area were accused of more widespread acts of pillaging. The British envoy stated: 'they [the French army] have heightened the most barbarous acts of licentious pillaging by their insolence ... [this] must show that the real intention of the French is to spread ruin and desolation over Germany' (Mitchell to Holdernesse, 1/2/58). The French army was restricted in its scope for pillaging as it withdrew after the Battle of Minden, since most of the countryside had already been stripped of supplies earlier in the campaign. Numerous villages were burned when civilians retaliated against the French pillaging attempts.

The central theater of operations' records yield additional anecdotes of the armies exacting damage upon the civilian population. A Prussian private soldier serving during the first Saxony campaign in 1756 noted that 'on the march every man thrust into his pack – it goes without saying on enemy territory – whatever he can lay his hands on' (Childs, *Armies and Warfare in Europe*, p. 164). The Prussians used Saxony as a forward military depot for operations throughout the war, and the principality suffered greatly as a result. The Austrians and especially the Prussians stripped the countryside bare each campaigning season. The Prussians also marched into neighboring German principalities to seek monetary contributions to the Prussian war effort, and to seize recruits to reinforce the decreasing Prussian army. The campaigns in Bohemia also took a heavy toll. Taxes had been raised in the Austrian provinces to support the war effort, and Bohemia, with its agricultural wealth, paid a heavier toll than most. To increase the burden, the Prussians made numerous forays into the province, pillaging and exacting contributions from the local population. After the Battle of Kolin, the Prussian army pillaged and destroyed villages to such an extent that, as recorded in the 'Austrian Journal', 'since the Prussians continue burning the villages through which they pass, Colonel Loudon has sent word to them that, if they persist in such actions, he will no longer give quarter to prisoners that he takes from them' (St Paul, *1757: The Defence of Prague*, p. 100).

Berlin was occupied twice and forced to pay contributions both times to the Russian/Austrian forces. The Cossacks of the

Russian army committed numerous atrocities against the Prussian populations in the Oder River area, and reports of these activities sparked the Prussian armies at Zorndorf and Kunersdorf to give no quarter to captured Russian soldiers. It has been estimated that a fifth of the population of the Prussian province of Pomerania was lost during the conflict, from atrocities committed as well as food shortages after the Russians pillaged the area. However, East Prussia was occupied by the Russians throughout the conflict and did not suffer such losses, largely due to the fact that it was not a scene of fighting after 1757.

There are also many examples of abuse of the civilian population during the war in North America. People living in the frontier regions were at risk from raids by the irregular forces of both sides. The French and their Native American allies were very successful, especially early in the war, at spreading terror along the frontier. The French-allied Native American attack on the garrison and civilians of Fort William Henry in the woods of the New York frontier went down in history as a massacre, and the French irregular activities led Amherst to declare in 1760: 'the French troops all lay down their arms and are not to serve during the war, their behaviour in carrying on a cruel and barbarous war in this country, I thought deserved this disgrace' (Amherst to General Joseph Yorke, 6/9/60). However, the British were capable of similar terror tactics. The French population of Acadia was forcibly deported to Louisiana; Roger's Rangers attacked the French-allied Native American settlement of St Francis, killing and capturing most of the population. During the battle for Quebec, Wolfe issued orders to lay waste the surrounding countryside. His motives were twofold: one was to draw the French out to battle, and the other was to destroy the Native American villages (Wolfe, *Instructions to Young Officers*, p. 81).

Similar situations arose in India. The French units, due to the fact that they were seldom paid, often pillaged the countryside for supplies and forage. As the British closed in on Pondicherry in 1761, orders were issued to pillage the countryside (Coote's Journal, II).

The war created economic problems for all the nations involved. It lasted longer than most states had anticipated. States such as Prussia and Austria had hoped for a short and decisive campaign in central Europe, while Great Britain and France expected that it would take longer, but still not as long as it did.

Many historians view Great Britain as the principal victor in the war. However, the British victories were very costly to the nation in terms of debt. The need to provide the sums to build up the fleet and keep armies in the field drove up spending considerably. An example of the costs: £1,968,477 was required to keep His Britannic Majesty's Army in the field in 1759 (*Naval and Military Memoirs*, Note 134), and this was only a fraction of the cost of the rest of the regular army and Royal Navy deployed overseas. Annual tax revenue for 1760 was £15 million, double the revenue of 1756, but there was still a shortfall and the state had to borrow to keep the war going. The national debt of Great Britain rose from £75 million in 1756 to £133 million in 1763.

Prussia, a small state by comparison to Great Britain, was also at the breaking point financially as a result of the war. The government had a reserve of 13 million talers at the beginning of the conflict. During the course of the war, taxation in Prussia reached 43 million talers, which was a heavy burden on the population. Frederick debased the currency of the state three times during the war, which created a further 29 million talers. He also included captured currency from his enemies in Saxony, Silesia, and Pomerania. Captured lands such as Saxony were stripped bare, which allowed him to raise 53 million talers. A major element of Frederick's economic policy was negotiation of the annual subsidy from Great Britain. Frederick had concluded a subsidy treaty with Britain on 11 April 1758, under which the British provided 27 million talers, which was a very substantial part of his overall war budget (Duffy, *Army of Frederick the Great*, pp. 95–99). When the leadership of the British government passed to Lord Bute in 1762, however, the annual subsidy ceased, creating further financial hardships for Prussia.

The war cost for Austria amounted to 392 million gulden. The original estimate of military expenditure per year had been 28 million gulden, and the annual military budget during wartime was three times the peacetime budget. The Austrians were clearly over budget, forcing the government to raise taxes. This accounted for 144 million gulden over the course of the war, the brunt of which was borne by the provinces of Austria and Bohemia, as noted previously. The

French subsidy to Austria was smaller in scale than the British subsidy to Prussia, amounting to only about 25 million gulden (Szabo, *Kaunitz and Enlightened Absolutism*, pp. 122–30). By 1760, France was having difficulty providing the annual subsidy of 12 million gulden as a result of problems caused by the loss of New France and most

of her commercial fleet. Austria had also promised a subsidy of 1 million rubles a year to Russia after they signed the First Treaty of Versailles, which became increasingly

Civilian cost – Austrian *Grenz* pillaging a village and killing any opposition. (Anne S. K. Brown Military Collection, Brown University Library)

difficult to maintain as the war progressed. Various assets of the royal treasury were sold off to gain revenue, but still debts continued to increase. The financial situation forced reductions in the officer corps by 1760. By the end of 1761, each regiment of the army had been reduced by two companies, and close to 12 percent of the army had been disbanded. Officers in Silesia were being paid with paper money that would be redeemable after the war had ended, ensuring that the debts and cost of the war would continue to plague Austria well into the future.

The Russians were able to provide for their war effort by the extreme harshness with which the various governmental organizations stripped the countryside of needed material and raised taxes on all levels of society. The actual system was not highly or centrally organized, which meant that corruption was widespread, especially in the countryside. The severe governmental regulations also provoked local serf uprisings, although these were put down quickly. Toward the end of the war, the lack of revenue was taking its toll on the war effort, and the Empress Elizabeth was quoted as saying that she would sell her diamonds and dresses, if necessary, to continue the war.

France, as mentioned above, also had economic difficulties. It cost the French state 24.5 million livres a year to field the French armies. The cost to maintain foreign troops in the field was 12.5 million livres a year, but at least the French state did not have to provide the fodder and supplies for the French army in Germany. That was provided by the various German states that had been occupied by or allied with France. Interest rates in France rose steadily as the government increased its borrowing. The French state had decided to finance the war effort by loans instead of raising taxes, but because of this decision the national

debt rose from 1,360 million livres in 1753 to 2,350 million livres in 1764 (Riley, *The Seven Years War and the Old Regime in France*, pp. 180–84). French defeats in the naval and colonial theaters affected trade overseas, and

No quarter given – Russian print of a skirmish between Cossacks and Prussian Dragoons. Note the image in the lower left corner, showing the apparent killing of a wounded Prussian Dragoon. (Anne S. K. Brown Military Collection, Brown University Library)

a massive shipbuilding program undertaken late in the war drove up spending even further. Commercial interests had to turn toward the continent to make up for the losses in the colonies, and with the loss of revenue from overseas, France's ability to make war proved to be limited. She had to halve her annual subsidy to Austria, and her troops in the field often suffered from lack of payment.

The nun's story

This is an account written by a French nun who was present at the siege and occupation of Quebec in 1759-60. No record of her name survives, nor is it known if she was from France or Canadian-born. We do know that she was a Sister at the General Hospital of Quebec, and that her Order had houses in both New and Old France. There is also no information given regarding her specific age, although from her references to the 'young sisters' one might guess that she was at least in her late 20s or early 30s.

Most of the nun's account deals with military events, and the effects upon herself, her convent, and the civilians of Quebec are discussed in relation to these. In writing her account of the events leading up to the British Siege of Quebec, the nun describes the steps that the French took to counter the British, and notes that they were hampered in disposition of troops by a shortage of men. The Canadian militia was called out, and troops were sent from Montreal to Quebec. Even so, there were not enough troops available to cover all of the areas requiring protection. Earlier in her account, the nun had described the fevers that had plagued the troops, from the arrival of the first soldiers from Old France in 1755. It is not clear what kind of fever this was, or if it had spread into the civilian population. These illnesses, along with the battle casualties of the previous three years' fighting, had taken their toll on the French troops, and they were not operating at full strength. This also testifies to the Royal Navy's highly effective blockade, which had consistently thwarted attempts by the French Navy to reinforce New France with men and supplies. It also enabled the British to seize positions on the south bank of the St. Lawrence River, just opposite Quebec. The first major bombardment of the town, as corroborated by this account, took place on 24 July.

The nun explains that the English bombardment took a serious toll on the town in short order. She describes the numbers of wounded people arriving for treatment at the convent, along with other civilians seeking refuge from the enemy bombardment in the convent complex, which at that point was outside the range of the British artillery. Before long, every shelter inside the convent's walls, including the stables, the attics, and the church itself, were filled with wounded and refugees. The arrival of nuns fleeing from two other convents in the area provided more hands to help with the sick and wounded, but put further strain on the limited food stores available. Of their privations, the nun says only that they were happy 'to partake with them [the refugee nuns] the little that remained to us.' The combination of the bombardment and blockade also brought the threat of famine to the town's beleaguered population. Buildings housing food and other stores were destroyed by artillery, along with much of the lower town. The situation became increasingly desperate.

The Battle of the Plains of Abraham, which took place on 13 September 1759, secured the British hold on Quebec—at least for the winter months. The nuns and refugees awaited the outcome of the battle inside the convent, trembling with dread and fear at the carnage taking place nearly under their windows. The nun describes how, overcome by what they saw, she and her sisters ventured onto the field of battle to try to assist the wounded and dying. When they realized that the tide of battle had turned definitively against France, she and the others tried to put their faith in God, but as she notes, 'the enemy, master of the country and at two paces from our House; exposed to the fury of the Soldier, we had everything to fear.' She notes with relief the subsequent arrival of a British officer, who reassured them that they were there only to use part of the convent grounds to help them hold the town against any French troops who still refused to capitulate.

With most of the town firmly in the hands of the British, the nun describes how the citizens tried to decide whether to surrender formally or to rally their diminished resources and try to fight on. Against those who did not wish to surrender, the Bourgeois, or merchants stated that they had sacrificed all their worldly goods and even their homes, but that 'they cannot resolve themselves to having their throats slit in front of their wives and children.' It seemed that without their support, the citizens would not fight on, and so they capitulated to the British.

The French made their formal surrender contingent upon the British agreeing to certain conditions, of which the nun cites two: the right to their religion, and the benefits accorded to citizens. Given that at this time the restrictions against Catholics in Great Britain and Ireland were severe, the concession allowing the French to continue to practice their religion was a significant

one, but she notes that the British agreed without hesitation. She also says, 'we could not without injustice complain of the fashion in which we were treated,' although she notes that they were obliged to lodge a guard of thirty British soldiers, who seized the convent's choir and helped themselves to the household goods, belonging to the parents of the convent's nuns, which had been stored there. More upsetting and annoying still, she complains, was having to listen to them continue their conversations throughout Mass.

The establishment of the British occupation government brought some return to normality, but the nun and her community faced the future with uncertainty. Their supplies were still short, and she laments that they had 'no wine, nor other refreshments to give' to the wounded. She and her fellow citizens conceded the supremacy of the British, but considered their oaths of loyalty an act of expediency only. In that winter of 1759-60, they had not given up hope that the French would ultimately recapture Quebec and that they, loyal French citizens, would remain part of the French empire.

Ramifications for the future

The Seven Years' War ended with the peace treaties of Paris and Hubertusburg. Prussia survived the war intact and escaped the threat of being dismembered by her enemies. She had lost 10 percent of her population and was economically on the verge of breakdown, but emerged with a great reputation. Following the war, Prussia could indisputably claim to be a major European power, on a par with Austria in terms of her influence and presence in the German Diet. Over the course of the next 100 years, Prussia eclipsed Austria as the major German state. The performance of the Prussian military in the face of such adversity led many to claim that it was the best in Europe. Numerous states including Great Britain, Russia, and France tried to adopt various Prussian models for their armies, notwithstanding Prussian military defeats and shortcomings. The deficiencies of the Prussian army were evident during the War of the Bavarian Succession (1778–79), 15 years after the Seven Years' War, and battlefield performance continued to decline throughout the rest of the century. The final humiliation came when the Prussians were soundly defeated by Napoleon at Jena in 1806.

France at the end of the war was a shell of her former self, beaten and embarrassed. Widespread military reform was indicated, but while many in France pushed for the Prussian models to be adopted, these were not without critics. The artillery was successfully reformed under the leadership of Jean de Baptiste Gribeauval during the 1760s, and would prove decisive in the later campaigns of the armies of the Revolution and Napoleon. The early attempts to form integrated and flexible columns led to the development of divisional structures for the army, and this in turn evolved to the higher levels, allowing commanders to control larger units of men over a given battlefield. Light infantry units were formally adopted in 1788, which meant that French units would march across territory with all arms represented within a divisional structure and with light infantry out in front to reconnoiter and harass the enemy as necessary.

The French navy replaced most of its losses in a major construction program, and the whole structure of the navy was reformed, from the standardization of armaments and vessels to the building of naval colleges. The French navy was a considerable threat for the Royal Navy during the American War of Independence. However, the debt caused by the war and the need for rearmament caused delays in the reform of the governmental administration, which was clearly needed. This mounting debt and the burden it placed upon the people of France was ultimately one of the causes of the French Revolution.

The war ended Austria's claim to Silesia. Maria Theresa realized that a military solution to the problem presented by Prussia was not viable, and Austria spent the next years dealing with internal reform of the state. Under the leadership of Kaunitz, the Austrian Empire became a more centralized state than had existed previously. There was also significant economic reform, and the debt was made more manageable under the various schemes established. By 1788 the revenue of the state had doubled and the debt was lower than that of the French and British governments.

The Russian state ended the war on a high note. Its armies had defeated the mighty Prussian army on several occasions. As with Austria, Russia turned away from confrontation with Prussia, choosing instead to attack the Ottoman lands in the Balkans, and she scored significant victories against the Turks. The Russian army finally began to reap the successes brought about by the reforms that had begun during the war. By the end of the century, Poland had disappeared from the European map as Austria, Prussia, and Russia cut her into pieces. Russia entered the Seven Years' War somewhat as an outsider. Due to her army's performance during the war and against the Turks, she began to be considered as a significant European power, and she has continued to play a central role in European international relations up to the present day.

While it would appear that Great Britain was the chief victor of the conflict, the war's costs were to have a more lasting impact than its victories. The army had performed well, but many lessons learned were quickly forgotten, as was apparent when the British army went to war in America in 1775 only 12 years later. Also, Britain became politically isolated from the rest of Europe. Under the Convention of Westminster, she had lost alliances with Russia and Austria, and the abandonment of Prussia during the last years of the war meant that Britain had no major allies on the continent.

The cost of war and the garrisoning of the newly won colonies caused Britain significant financial problems, and the British government alienated the 13 North

American colonies when it closed the lands newly gained by the Treaty of Paris to colonial settlers. The colonies felt they had a right to settle in these areas, and were annoyed further when the British government stipulated that the colonies pay for part of the protection that was now necessary in the region. Since the British government could not tax the colonists directly, it began instead to levy import duties on items. The Stamp Act of 1765 was the beginning of soured relations between the British and the colonists, and the Quebec Act of 1774 led to a further deterioration. This Act, which granted certain rights to the French Canadian settlers for their religion, Catholicism, as well as administration of the new lands of the Ohio valley, incensed the 13 colonies, and by 1775 they were in open rebellion against the British. By 1778, the French were actively supporting the American rebels. Some observers have contended that their motivation was partially the desire to inflict a defeat on the British and regain some of the face lost during the Seven Years' War. By 1783 Britain had lost the 13 colonies and had switched her attention to India, the centerpiece of what was to become the Second British Empire.

Further reading

Primary sources

Manuscript sources
British Library
Orme Collection
Haldimand Papers
Bouquet Papers
Clive Papers
Hardwicke Papers
Napier Papers
Howe Papers
Mss Eur B248 Fortunate Englishman
Mss Eur F190 Vols I–II Journal of Sir Eyre
   Coote
Mss Eur F128 Brigadier John Carnac
Mss King's 235 Marshal Contades
Add 11813 Captain William Parry (RN)
   Louisbourg

National Army Museum
5902–46 Attack on St Malo
6807–129 Capture of Manila
6807–142-13 Letter of an officer regarding
   the Battle of Minden
7506–26 Journal of the Allied Armies
   Marches from the 1st Arrival of British
   Troops in Germany to the Present Time
1762, John Tory
7508–47 Letter of an officer of Draper's
   Regiment at the Battle of Wandiwash
7510–92 Letter from an officer to his mother
   (Battle of Minden)

Public Record Office
Amherst Papers

Printed sources
Annual Register, 1762.
*A Soldiers Journal containing a particular
   description of the several descents on the
   French Coast*, London, 1770.
'General Orders in Wolfe's Army,' *Manuscripts
   Relating to the Early History of Canada*,
   Quebec, 1875.

*Naval and Military Memoirs of Great Britain
   1727–1783*, London, 1790.
'Reflections on the General Principles of War
   and on the Compositions and Characters
   of the Different Armies in Europe,'
   A. Lloyd, *Annual Register*, 1766.
'To Mr Davenport being the letters of Major
   Richard Davenport,' *Society for Army
   Historical Research*, London, 1968.
Bisset, A. (ed.), *Memoirs and Papers of Sir
   Andrew Mitchell*, London, 1850.
Bougainville, Louis Antoine de, *Adventure
   in the Wilderness*, Norman, Oklahoma,
   1964.
Bradstreet, J., *Impartial Account of Lt Colonel
   Bradstreet's Expedition to Fort Frontenac*,
   London, 1759.
Dalrymple, C., *Military Essay containing
   reflections of the raising, arming, clothing
   and Discipline of British Cavalry and
   Infantry*, London, 1761.
Dundas, Sir David, *Principles of Military
   Movement*, London, 1788.
Frederick II, *History of the Seven Years War by
   Frederick the Great*, translated by Thomas
   Holcroft, London, 1789.
Frederick II, *Military Instructions written by the
   King of Prussia for the Generals of his Army*,
   London, 1762.
Frederick II, *Regulations for the Prussian
   Infantry and Cavalry*, London, 1757.
Hamilton, C. (ed.), *Braddock's Defeat: Journal
   of Captain Robert Chomley's Batman;
   Journal of a British Officer; Halkett's Orderly
   Book*, Norman, Oklahoma, 1959.
Knox, H., *Historical Journal of Campaigns in
   North America, 1757–1760*, New York,
   1914.
Lloyd, H., *History of the Late War in Germany*,
   London, 2 vols, 1766–81.
Luvaas, Jay (ed.), *Fredrick the Great on the Art
   of War*, London, 1966.

Orme, E., *History of the Military Transactions of the British Nation in Indostan*, London, 1763.

Pouchot, P., *Memoir of the Late War in North America between the French and the English*, Roxbury, Mass., 1864.

St Paul, H., *1757: The Defence of Prague: Journal of Horace St Paul*, edited by Neil Cogswell, Northampton, England, 1998.

Wolfe, J., *Instructions to Young Officers*, London, 1768.

Yorke, P.C. (ed.), *Life and Correspondence of Phillip Yorke, Earl of Hardwick*, Cambridge, 1913.

Secondary sources

Balisch, A., 'Infantry Battlefield Tactics in the 18th Century,' *Studies in History and Politics* 83–84.

Beranger, J., *History of the Hapsburg Empire*, London, 1997.

Childs, J., *Armies and Warfare in Europe*, Manchester, 1982.

Dann, U., *Hanover and England 1740–1760: Diplomacy and Survival*, Leicester, 1991.

Duffy, C., *Army of Frederick the Great*, 2nd edn, Chicago, 1996.

Duffy, C., *Army of Maria Theresa*, North Pomfret, Vermont, 1977.

Duffy, C., *Russia's Military Way to the West*, London, 1981.

Edwardes, M., *Battle of Plassey and the Conquest of Bengal*, London, 1963.

Fortescue, Sir John, *History of the British Army*, Vol. II, London, 1908.

Harper, J. R., *78th Fighting Fraser's in Canada*, Montreal, 1966.

Houlding, J. A., *Fit for Service: Training of the British Army*, Oxford, 1981.

Hughes, B. O., *Open Fire: Artillery Tactics from Marlborough to Wellington*, Chichester, England, 1983.

Kaplan, H., *Russia and the Outbreak of the Seven Years War*, Berkeley, California, 1968.

Keep, J., *Soldiers of the Tsar: Army and Society in Russia*, Oxford, 1985.

Kennett, L., *French Armies in the Seven Years' War*, Durham, North Carolina, 1967.

Mackesy, P., *Coward of Minden*, London, 1979.

Marcus, G., *Quiberon Bay: The Campaign in Home Waters*, London, 1960.

Middleton, R., *Bells of Victory: Pitt–Newcastle Ministry and Conduct of the Seven Years' War*, Cambridge, 1985.

Nosworthy, B., *Anatomy of Victory: Battle Tactics 1689–1763*, Hippocrene, New York, 1992.

Paret, P. (ed.), *Frederick the Great: A Profile*, New York, 1972.

Paret, P., *Yorck and the Era of Prussian Reform*, Princeton, New Jersey, 1966.

Pritchard, J. S., *Louis XV's Navy, 1748–1762*, Kingston, Ontario, 1987.

Riley, J., *The Seven Years' War and the Old Regime in France: Economic and Financial Toll*, Princeton, New Jersey, 1986.

Savory, R., *His Britannic Majesty's Army in Germany*, Oxford, 1966.

Schweizer, K., *England, Prussia and the Seven Years' War: Studies in Alliance Policies and Diplomacy*, Lewiston, New York, 1989.

Showalter, D., *Wars of Frederick the Great*, London, 1996.

Szabo, F., *Kaunitz and Enlightened Absolutism, 1753–1780*, Cambridge, 1994.

Unpublished thesis

Marston, D., 'Swift and Bold: The 60th Royal American Regiment and Warfare in North America, 1755–1765,' MA thesis, McGill University, 1997.

Index

Figures in **bold** refer to illustrations